LUXURY HOUSES

SEASIDE

LUXURY HOUSES

SEASIDE

edited by Cristina Paredes Benítez

teNeues

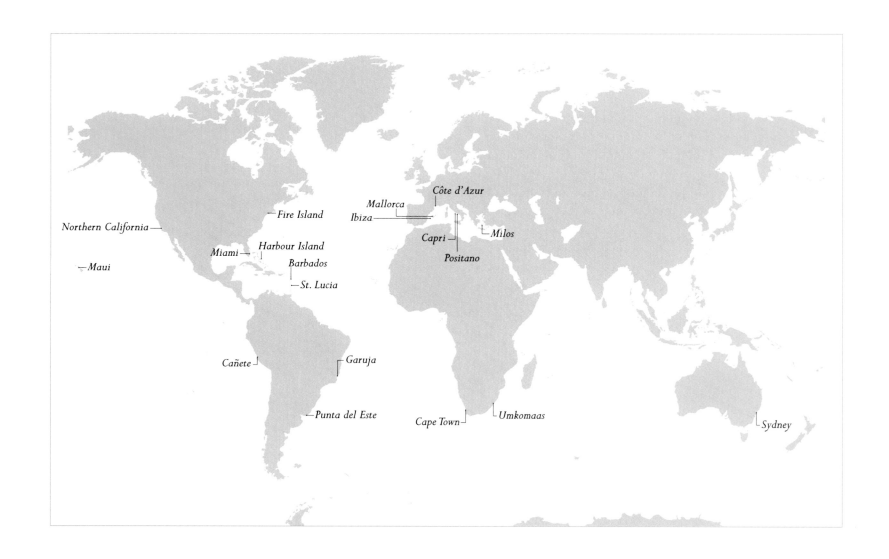

Northern California

Fire Island

Mallorca

Côte d'Azur

Ibiza

Miami

Harbour Island

Capri

Milos

Maui

Barbados

Positano

St. Lucia

Cañete

Garuja

Punta del Este

Cape Town

Umkomaas

Sydney

Luxury Houses

SEASIDE

Introduction

Coastal areas have attracted villagers since days gone by thanks to a good climate and the sea's natural offerings. The fishing industry and trade have transformed coastal settlements into growth areas with social and economic development. On the other hand, the sea is one of the most beautiful natural elements from whose spell no one escapes. A storm can provoke fear or emotions, whereas the goodness of a calm sea can relax and warm the spirit. Moreover the beach and the sea evoke images of peace and rest. The sea is an element awash with magnetism which awakens a multitude of sensations, it be heavenly beaches or abrupt Atlantic coastlines. The houses in this book are inhabited by people who have decided to live next to the sea and make it an integral part of their lives.

In this book we present magnificent dwellings from all over the world, highlighted for their elegance and coastal location. These coastal residences can be very diverse, ranging from magnificent villas to splendid and luxurious beach houses. They all possess state-of-the-art architecture and excellent interiors, be they holiday homes or habitual residences. The styles are varied, such as a sizeable neoclassic residence or a cozy oriental inspired house situated in a Majorcan cove. Here, elegant and exclusive architecture is blended into a setting of outstanding beauty. The impressive views play an important role in these villas due to the undeniable link between architecture and surroundings. The interiors are all of a high quality, adapted to harmonize with the personality of the owners. There are classic Mediterranean style residences as well as modern villas. The luxurious air of these homes is complemented by maritime surroundings, architectural design and the decoration and quality of materials. The ideal combination of all these elements can result in fantastic villas with a sumptuous yet relaxed atmosphere. Magnificence and elegance are the key words.

Einleitung

Die Küste war schon von jeher der perfekte Siedlungsort für viele Völker, zum einen, weil das Klima so mild ist, zum anderen, weil das Meer den Menschen vieles zu bieten hat. Seit langer Zeit schon trugen der Fischfang und der Handel zum Wachstum und zur wirtschaftlichen und sozialen Entwicklung der Küstengebiete bei. Auch besitzt das Meer eine Schönheit und Anziehungskraft, die niemanden unberührt lässt. Die Kraft eines Sturmes erregt Furcht in den Menschen, die Windstille über einem ruhigen Meer entspannt und erfreut die Seele. Strand und Meer erwecken in den Menschen stets Bilder von Frieden und Ruhe. Egal, ob es sich um paradiesische Strände oder schroffe Atlantikküsten handelt, das Meer ist immer ein Element voller Anziehungskraft, das viele Empfindungen in uns wachruft. Die Häuser und Wohnungen in diesem Band gehören Menschen, die eines Tages beschlossen haben, am Meer zu leben und dieses zu einem Bestandteil ihres Lebens zu machen.

In diesem Buch werden viele Häuser auf der ganzen Welt vorgestellt, deren Gemeinsamkeiten in ihrer Eleganz und der Lage am Meer bestehen. Es handelt sich um sehr verschiedene Haustypen an der Küste, wie zum Beispiel um herrschaftliche Villen oder luxuriöse, prachtvolle Strandhäuser. Manchmal sind es Ferienhäuser oder auch der ständige Wohnsitz einer Familie, und allen ist die beeindruckende Architektur und gelungene Innengestaltung gemein. Die Stile, die vorgestellt werden, sind sehr unterschiedlich, sowohl neoklassische Häuser als auch einladende Gebäude im orientalischen Stil in einer Bucht in Mallorca werden in diesem Buch gezeigt. Die elegante und exklusive Architektur verschmilzt mit der ungewöhnlich schönen Umgebung. Der beeindruckende Ausblick spielt eine wichtige Rolle in diesen Villen, da die enge Beziehung zwischen der Architektur und der umgebenden Natur von großer Bedeutung ist. All diese Häuser zeichnen sich durch ihre edle Einrichtung aus, und sie zeigen die Persönlichkeit ihrer Bewohner. Es werden sowohl Wohnhäuser im klassischen Mittelmeerstil als auch moderne Villen gezeigt. Diese Häuser sind luxuriös und werden außerdem noch durch ihre Lage am Meer geprägt sowie durch die Architektur, Dekoration und die edlen Materialien, die verwendet wurden. Durch die gelungene Kombination all dieser Elemente entstanden wunderschöne Villen, in denen man eine entspannte und luxuriöse Atmosphäre genießen kann. Die vorgestellten Häuser kann man perfekt mit den Worten Pracht und Eleganz charakterisieren.

Introduction

De tous temps, le littoral marin à été un emplacement parfait pour accueillir de nombreux villages, tant en raison des bienfaits du climat que pour les ressources naturelles offertes par la mer. Depuis des temps immémoriaux, la pêche et le commerce ont transformé les territoires côtiers en centres de croissance et de développement économique et social. La mer est également l'un des éléments naturels les plus beaux, ne laissant personne indifférent. La force d'une tempête peut provoquer la peur ou l'émotion, et les bienfaits d'une mer calme détendent et animent l'esprit. En outre, les bords de mer ont toujours évoqué des images de paix et de repos : plages paradisiaques ou côtes abruptes de l'Atlantique, la mer est chargée de magnétisme, provoquant une foule de sensations. Les demeures selectionnées pour cet ouvrage sont occupées par des personnes ayant décidé de vivre près de la mer, pour l'intégrer à leur vie.

Ce livre recueille une sélection de maisons du monde entier, caractérisées par leur élégance et leur emplacement au bord de la mer. Ces résidences côtières, des magnifiques villas aux luxueuses résidences sur la plage, peuvent revêtir des typologies bien diverses. Pensées comme demeure principale ou pour jouir des vacances, ces maisons affichent une architecture magnifique et une décoration d'intérieur de grande qualité. Les styles sont variés, ils vont d'une très vaste résidence néoclassique à une accueillante maison de style oriental dans une crique de Majorque. L'architecture élégante et exclusive fusionne avec l'environnement d'une beauté exceptionnelle, et les vues impressionnantes prennent la vedette dans tous les cas. En effet, l'étroite relation entre l'architecture et son cadre prend içi toute son importance. Les intérieurs, toujours de grande qualité, se sont adaptés à la personnalité des propriétaires : on y trouve autant de résidences de style méditerranéen classique que de villas modernes. Au luxe que respirent ces demeures s'ajoute l'environnement marin, le concept architectural, la décoration et la qualité des matériaux. La combinaison réussie de tous ces éléments engendre de fantastiques demeures où profiter d'une atmosphère détendue et somptueuse. Magnificence et élégance décrivent parfaitement les projets çi-présentés.

Introducción

El litoral ha sido desde tiempos remotos la ubicación perfecta para muchos pueblos, ya sea por la bonanza del clima o por los recursos naturales que ofrece el mar. Desde tiempos inmemoriales, la pesca y el comercio han transformado los territorios costeros en núcleos de crecimiento y desarrollo económico y social. Por otro lado, el mar es uno de los elementos naturales de más belleza, y que a nadie deja indiferente. La fuerza de una tempestad puede provocar temor o emoción y la bonanza de un mar en calma puede relajar y alegrar el espíritu. Además, la playa y el mar siempre evocan imágenes de paz y descanso: ya sea en playas paradisíacas o en abruptas costas atlánticas, el mar es un elemento lleno de magnetismo que despierta multitud de sensaciones. Las viviendas de este volumen están habitadas por personas que decidieron en su día habitar junto al mar y convertirlo en parte integrante de su vida.

Este libro recoge una selecta muestra de casas de todo el mundo caracterizadas por su elegancia y por su emplazamiento cerca del mar. Estas residencias situadas en la costa pueden ser de tipología muy diversa: desde magníficas villas hasta espléndidas y lujosas casas junto a la playa. Pensadas para disfrutar de las vacaciones o como residencia habitual, estas viviendas muestran una magnífica arquitectura y un excelente interiorismo. Los estilos son variados, e incluyen desde una amplísima residencia neoclásica hasta una acogedora casa de estilo oriental en una cala de Mallorca. La arquitectura elegante y exclusiva se fusiona con un entorno de excepcional belleza. Las impresionantes vistas desempeñan un papel muy importante en estas villas, pues la estrecha relación que se establece entre arquitectura y entorno cobra una gran relevancia. Los interiores son siempre de gran calidad y se han adaptado a la personalidad de los propietarios; se pueden encontrar tanto residencias de estilo mediterráneo clásico como modernas villas. Al lujo que se respira en estas viviendas se suma el entorno marítimo, el diseño de la arquitectura, la decoración y la calidad de los materiales. La acertada combinación de todos estos elementos da como resultado fantásticas villas en las que se puede disfrutar de un ambiente relajado y suntuoso. Magnificencia y elegancia describen a la perfección los proyectos que se muestran a continuación.

Introduzione

Sin da tempi remoti il litorale è stata la zona di insediamento preferita da molti popoli sia per via del clima benevolo che per le varie risorse naturali offerte dal mare. Sin dall'antichità la pesca ed il commercio hanno trasformato i territori costieri in nuclei di crescita e sviluppo sia economico che sociale. D'altro canto, il mare è uno degli elementi naturali più affascinanti che non lascia indifferente nessuno. La forza di una tempesta può provocare timore e suscitare forti emozioni così come la vista di un mare calmo può far rilassare e rallegrare lo spirito. A tutto ciò si aggiunge il fatto che la spiaggia e il mare evocano sempre immagini di pace e relax. Sia che si tratti di spiagge paradisiache o di scoscese coste atlantiche, il mare è un elemento pieno di magnetismo in grado di suscitare le più svariate sensazioni. Le case di questo volume sono abitate da persone che in un determinato momento hanno deciso di vivere accanto al mare e di convertirlo in una parte integrante della loro vita.

Questo libro comprende un'accurata selezione di case di tutto il mondo caratterizzate dalla loro eleganza e dalla loro posizione vicino al mare. Le varie residenze, tutte situate in zone costiere, possono essere di tipologie ben diverse: da magnifiche ville fino a splendide mansioni di lusso a due passi dal mare. Concepite come luogo di villeggiatura dove godersi le vacanze o come residenza abituale, queste abitazioni mostrano un'eccellente realizzazione architettonica e pregevoli esempi di arredamento degli interni. Gli stili e le ubicazioni sono vari, e vanno da una grande dimora neoclassica fino ad un'accogliente casa in stile orientale in una cala di Maiorca. L'architettura, singolare ed elegante, si fonde alla perfezione con l'ambiente circostante, di eccezionale bellezza. Anche le magnifiche viste che si godono dalla maggior parte di queste ville sono un altro dei loro tratti caratteristici, che rafforza il loro rapporto con il territorio che le accoglie. Gli interni sono sempre di grande qualità e rispecchiano i gusti e la personalità dei proprietari; si possono trovare sia residenze in stile mediterraneo classico che ville moderne. Al lusso e all'eleganza di queste dimore va aggiunta anche la tipica atmosfera marittima, la ricercatezza e la qualità dei materiali di costruzione. La giusta combinazione di tutti questi elementi dà come risultato delle ville fantastiche dove poter godere di un ambiente rilassato ed accogliente. Sontuosità ed eleganza sono altri due fattori che accomunano i progetti descritti di seguito in questo volume.

Waley House

Sydney, Australia

This residence is a take on the traditional houses built next to the beach on the Palm Beach coast. Not only does it capture its original essence, but it also serves as an alternative to the modern constructions that degrade the natural surroundings. The stylish interior has an oriental air where simplicity is the key without detracting from the elegant and modern style. The spaciousness and sizeable openings provide amazing sea views from the interior. Given the owners love of tai-chi it was important to enhance the connection between interior and exterior in order to create a favorable space in which to practice.

Dieses Wohnhaus ist eine Neuinterpretation traditioneller Häuser, so wie sie früher am Strand von Palm Beach errichtet wurden. Der Originalstil des Hauses wurde wiederhergestellt und so entstand ein Gegengewicht zu den modernen Bauten, die die Landschaft stören. Das elegante Innere ist im orientalischen Stil gestaltet, einfach, aber doch elegant und modern. Die großen Räume und Fenster lassen den Blick auf das Meer frei. Man suchte bewusst diese Verbindung zwischen innen und außen, da der Eigentümer hier Tai-Chi praktizieren wollte, eine seiner Lieblingsbeschäftigungen.

Cette résidence offre une nouvelle interprétation des maisons traditionnelles construites au bord de la plage de la côte de Palm Beach. Non seulement recouvre-t-elle son essence originelle mais elle s'offre également en contrepoint aux constructions dégradant le cadre naturel. L'intérieur élégant évoque le style oriental où prédomine une simplicité qui n'est pas exempte de classe et de modernité. Les amples espaces et les vastes ouvertures permettent de jouir des vues de la mer depuis l'intérieur. Cette connexion entre l'intérieur et l'extérieur a été recherchée expressément afin de favoriser la pratique du taï-chi, l'une des grandes passions du propriétaire.

Esta residencia es una reinterpretación de las casas tradicionales construidas junto a la playa de la costa de Palm Beach; no sólo recupera su esencia original sino que constituye un contrapunto a las modernas construcciones que degradan el entorno natural. El elegante interior evoca un estilo oriental y en él predomina una sencillez no exenta de clase y modernidad. Los espacios amplios y las grandes aberturas permiten disfrutar de las vistas al mar desde el interior. Se ha buscado esta conexión entre interior y exterior de forma expresa para favorecer la práctica del Tai Chi, una de las grandes aficiones del propietario.

Questa residenza è una reinterpretazione delle case tradizionali costruite vicino alla spiaggia della costa di Palm Beach; non solo recupera la sua essenza originaria ma costituisce un contrappunto alle moderne costruzioni che degradano l'ambiente dei dintorni. Gli interni eleganti evocano uno stile orientale e in essi predomina una semplicità non priva di una certa classe e dei tocchi di modernità. Gli ampi spazi e le grandi aperture consentono di godere dall'interno della vista del mare. Questo stretto rapporto tra l'interno e l'esterno dell'abitazione è stato fortemente voluto per agevolare la pratica del Tai Chi, uno degli hobby preferiti del proprietario.

Architect: Tim Roberts
Photographer: © Sharrin Rees

The exterior of the house and the surrounding vegetation give the residence the feel of a seaside cabin. On the upper floor, a spacious terrace provides the ideal place from where to enjoy the ocean views without interruption thanks to its transparency and simplicity. The wooden floor and the rays of sun which flood the spaces bring warmth to the ambience.

Die Fassade des Hauses und die umgebende Vegetation lassen es wie eine Hütte am Meer wirken. Von einer großen, transparenten und einfachen Terrasse im Obergeschoss aus blickt man ohne visuelle Hindernisse auf das Meer. Das Holz des Bodens und die Sonnenstrahlen, die die Räume durchfluten, lassen die Wohnumgebung sehr warm wirken.

L'extérieur de la demeure et la végétation la ceignant évoquent l'image d'une cabane au bord de la mer. Au niveau supérieur, une belle terrasse permet de contempler l'océan presque sans obstacles par sa transparence et sa simplicité. Le bois des parquets et les rayons du soleil qui inondent les espaces génèrent une ambiance chaleureuse.

El exterior de la vivienda y la vegetación circundante evocan la imagen de una cabaña junto al mar. En el piso superior, una amplia terraza permite contemplar el océano sin apenas obstáculos, gracias a su transparencia y sencillez. La madera del suelo y los rayos de sol que inundan los espacios proporcionan calidez al ambiente.

L'esterno dell'abitazione e la vegetazione dei dintorni evocano l'immagine di una capanna accanto al mare. Al piano superiore trova spazio un'ampia terrazza che grazie alla sua trasparenza e semplicità permette di ammirare l'oceano senza alcun ostacolo. Il legno del pavimento e i raggi di sole che inondano gli spazi rendono l'ambiente ancora più caldo e accogliente.

16 Waley House *Sydney, Australia*

The two Buddha statues are testament to the peculiar decorative style which defines this residence. The simplicity of the furniture and the opening up of the spaces outside make this a calm and natural setting.

Die beiden Buddhastatuen zeigen den besonderen Dekorationsstil dieses Hauses. Die Möbel sind einfach und die großen Fenster lassen die Umgebung friedlich und im Gleichgewicht mit der Natur wirken, die hier die Hauptrolle spielt.

Les deux statues de Bouddha affichent le style décoratif particulier définissant cette résidence. La simplicité du mobilier et l'ouverture sur l'extérieur font que l'ambiance sereine et le cadre naturel soient maîtres des lieux.

Las dos estatuas de Buda muestran el peculiar estilo decorativo que distingue a esta residencia, la sencillez del mobiliario y la abertura del espacio al exterior hacen que el ambiente de calma y el entorno natural sean los protagonistas.

Le due statue di Budda sono un esempio dello stile decorativo che definisce questa residenza; la semplicità della mobilia apporta ulteriore calma a uno spazio strettamente connesso con l'ambiente naturale dei dintorni.

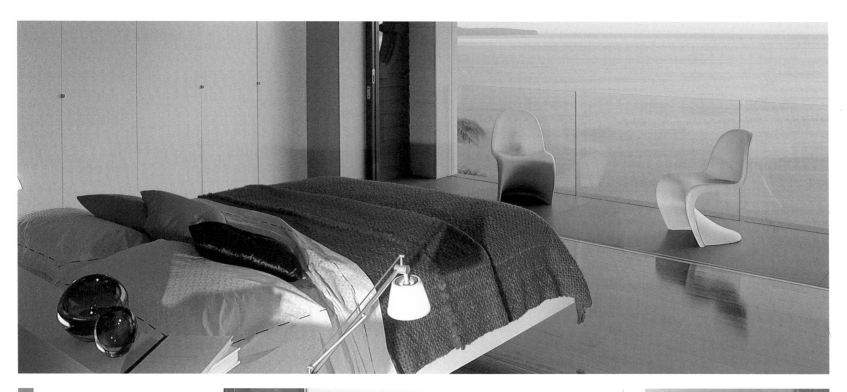

Guest House by the Sea

Harbour Island, The Bahamas

This residence, built to house the family's guests, offers the same luxuries and comforts as the main residence. Its beachfront location and luminous elegant interiors, with colonial style decoration, makes this a paradisiacal place set in beautiful surroundings. The wood, the majority of which is painted white, contrasts well with the colorful exterior and brings warmth to the rooms of distinct styles. The lamps, photographs, upholstery and the furniture have been carefully selected to create a refined colonial ambience.

Dieses Haus wurde eigens für die Gäste der Familie errichtet, und es ist genauso luxuriös und komfortabel wie das Haupthaus. Die eleganten und hellen Räume sind im Kolonialstil dekoriert und es liegt direkt am Strand in einer wundervollen Umgebung, ein wirklich paradiesischer Ort. Das Holz ist größtenteils weiß gestrichen, so dass ein Kontrast zu der bunten Umgebung entsteht und gleichzeitig eine freundliche Atmosphäre geschaffen wird. Die Räume sind in einem einheitlichen Stil ausgestattet. Die Lampen, Fotografien, Stoffe und die Möbel wurden sorgfältig ausgewählt, so dass ein edles Ambiente im Kolonialstil entstand.

Cette maison, conçue pour accueillir les invités de la famille, offre les mêmes luxes et conforts que la résidence principale. Les intérieurs sont élégants et lumineux, dotés d'une décoration de style colonial ; la situation au pied de la plage et la superbe du cadre naturel sont paradisiaques. Le bois, peint essentiellement en blanc, contraste avec la couleur extérieure et apporte sa chaleur aux pièces, décorées selon le même thème. Les lampes, photographies, toiles et mobilier ont été choisis avec soin pour créer une ambiance coloniale raffinée.

Esta residencia, construida para acoger a los invitados de la familia, ofrece los mismos lujos y comodidades que la vivienda principal. Los interiores son elegantes y luminosos, con una decoración de estilo colonial, y la ubicación a pie de playa, junto con la belleza del entorno, transportan a un lugar paradisíaco. La madera, pintada en su mayor parte de blanco, contrasta con el colorido del exterior y aporta calidez a las estancias, decoradas con un estilo unitario. Las lámparas, las fotografías, las telas y el mobiliario han sido cuidadosamente escogidos para crear un ambiente colonial refinado.

Questa dependance, costruita per alloggiare gli eventuali ospiti della famiglia, offre gli stessi comfort dell'abitazione principale. Gli interni sono eleganti e luminosi, con un arredamento in stile coloniale; l'invidiabile posizione, a pochi metri dalla spiaggia, assieme alla bellezza del paesaggio, fanno di questo un luogo paradisiaco. Il legno, dipinto per la maggior parte di bianco, contrasta con i colori accesi dell'esterno e conferisce calore alle varie stanze, arredate con uno stile unitario. Le fotografie, le lampade, le stoffe e i mobili sono stati scelti con la massima cura al fine di creare un ambiente coloniale di estrema eleganza.

Architect: The owners
Photographer: © M. Arnaud / Inside / Cover

The layout of the furniture in the living room is almost symmetrical and creates a comfortable and ample space. The whiteness and warmth of the wood give the room a lavish yet refreshing atmosphere.

Die Anordnung der Möbel im Wohnzimmer ist fast symmetrisch, der Raum ist komfortabel und großzügig geschnitten. Die Farbe Weiß und die Wärme des verwendeten Holzes schaffen eine frische und luxuriöse Atmosphäre.

La disposition du mobilier du salon presque symétrique crée un espace confortable et ample. Le blanc et la chaleur du bois confèrent à la pièce une atmosphère rafraîchissante et somptueuse.

La disposición del mobiliario en el salón es casi simétrica, y crea un espacio confortable y amplio. El blanco y la calidez de la madera otorgan a la estancia una atmósfera refrescante y suntuosa.

La disposizione della mobilia nel salone è quasi simmetrica, e crea uno spazio ampio e confortevole. Il bianco e i toni caldi del legno conferiscono alla stanza un'atmosfera rinfrescante e sontuosa.

The sea is the central theme of the decoration. *For example, the sea shells collected from the beach that are placed by a small desk and the maritime photos and maps on the wall accentuate the marine feel of the house.*

Viele der Dekorationselemente *spielen auf das Meer an, so zum Beispiel die Sammlung von Meeresschnecken und Muscheln neben dem kleinen Schreibtisch und die Fotografien und nautischen Karten an den Wänden. Diese Elemente unterstreichen den von der Küste geprägten Charakter des Hauses.*

Une foule de détails décoratifs *se réfèrent à la mer : ainsi, à côté d'un petit secrétaire, se trouve une collection de conques et de coquillages recueillis sur la plage, et sur les murs sont accrochées des photographies et cartes maritimes qui accentuent l'ambiance de la maison.*

Muchos detalles decorativos *hacen referencia al mar: por ejemplo, junto a un pequeño escritorio, hay una colección de caracolas y conchas que se han recogido de la playa, y de las paredes cuelgan fotografías y cartas marítimas que acentúan el ambiente marinero de la vivienda.*

Molti particolari decorativi *fanno riferimento al mare: per esempio, accanto ad una piccola scrivania, vi è una collezione di chiocciole di mare e conchiglie raccolte in spiaggia, e alle pareti sono appese varie fotografie e carte nautiche che accentuano l'ambiente marinaro dell'abitazione.*

House in Harbour Island

Harbour Island, The Bahamas

This splendid residence situated in the Bahamas manifests distinction and luxury in every corner. The large sized rooms and private access to the beach are just two examples of its grandeur. The color white is apparent in every room of the house, extending great luminosity. The wooden furniture brings warmth and elegance and the decorative objects, such as paintings, souvenirs and photographs are displayed in the living room and bedrooms creating a unitary style throughout the house. It is a captivating and distinguished villa where an elegant colonial style has been achieved through an attentive decoration.

Dieses Haus auf den Bahamas ist sehr edel und luxuriös eingerichtet. Die großen Räume und der private Zugang zum Strand sind nur zwei Beispiele für den großen Luxus. Überall in den Licht durchfluteten Räumen findet man die Farbe Weiß. Die Holzmöbel wirken sehr warm und elegant, und die Dekorationsobjekte wie Gemälde, Reiseandenken und Fotografien, die im Wohnzimmer und in den Schlafzimmern hängen, schaffen eine einheitliche Umgebung im ganzen Haus. In diesem eleganten Haus im Kolonialstil wusste man eine bezaubernde und sehr edle Atmosphäre zu schaffen, indem wirklich auf jedes Detail Wert gelegt wurde.

Cette splendide résidence située aux Bahamas affiche distinction et luxe jusque dans chaque recoin. Les grandes salles et l'accès privé à la plage ne sont que deux éléments de sa magnificence. Le blanc est présent dans chaque pièce de la demeure, apportant une grande luminosité. Le mobilier de bois est chaleureux et élégant, et les objets décoratifs comme par exemple tableaux, souvenirs de voyage et photographies se répartissent entre le salon et les chambres à coucher pour créer un style uni à travers toute la maison. En définitive, il s'agit d'un lieu captivant et distingué, où chaque détail a été soigné pour assurer un style colonial élégant.

Esta espléndida residencia situada en las Bahamas muestra distinción y lujo en cada rincón. Las grandes salas y el acceso privado a la playa son solo dos ejemplos de su magnificencia. El blanco está presente en todas las estancias de la vivienda y proporciona una gran luminosidad. El mobiliario de madera aporta calidez y elegancia, y los objetos decorativos, como cuadros, recuerdos de viajes y fotografías, se reparten entre el salón y los dormitorios creando un estilo unitario en toda la casa. En definitiva, se trata de una villa cautivadora y distinguida, en la que se han cuidado todos los detalles para conseguir un elegante estilo colonial.

Questa splendida dimora situata alle Bahamas sprizza distinzione e lusso da tutte le parti. Le grandi sale e l'accesso privato alla spiaggia sono soltanto due esempi della sua magnificenza. Il bianco è presente in tutte le stanze dell'abitazione e ne aumenta la luminosità. I mobili in legno si caratterizzano per i toni caldi e lo stile elegante; gli oggetti di arredo, quali quadri, souvenir di viaggi e fotografie si distribuiscono tra il salone e le camere da letto creando uno stile unitario in tutta la casa. In definitiva, si tratta di una villa incantevole e signorile, dove tutto è stato curato nei minimi particolari al fine di ottenere un elegante stile coloniale.

Interior design: India Hicks, David Flint Wood
Photographer: © M. Arnaud / Inside / Cover

The vegetation which surrounds the property and its closeness to the sea make this residence a paradisiacal place. To the right, a magnificently reproduced sailing boat dominates one of the corners of the living room, revealing the owners' close relationship with the sea.

Die Vegetation, die das Grundstück umgibt, und die Nähe des Meeres machen dieses Haus zu einem paradiesischen Ort. Auf der rechten Seite nimmt eine wundervolle Reproduktion eines Segelschiffes, die das enge Verhältnis der Eigentümer zum Meer beweist, eine beherrschende Position ein.

La végétation ceignant la propriété et sa proximité avec la mer en font un lieu paradisiaque. À droite, une magnifique reproduction de voilier préside à l'un des angles du salon et rappelle l'intime relation des propriétaires avec la mer.

La vegetación que rodea la finca y su proximidad con el mar hacen de esta residencia un lugar paradisíaco. A la derecha, una magnífica reproducción de un velero preside uno de los rincones del salón y muestra la estrecha relación de los propietarios con el mar.

La vegetazione che circonda la tenuta e la sua posizione, in prossimità del mare, fanno di questa casa un luogo paradisiaco. Sulla destra, una magnifica riproduzione di un veliero presiede uno degli angoli del salone e mostra lo stretto rapporto dei proprietari con il mare.

The living room is a space decorated with elegance and forethought. The chimney provides warmth on cold nights, the sofas and armchairs make for comfortable areas for relaxation.

Der Salon ist sehr sorgsam und elegant eingerichtet. Der Kamin spendet in den kalten Nächten Wärme, und die Sofas und Sessel bilden komfortable Winkel, in denen man die Momente der Ruhe genießen kann.

Le salon est un espace décoré avec soin et élégance. La cheminée offre sa chaleur lors des nuits froides et les sofas et fauteuils forment de confortables recoins où jouir des moments de repos.

El salón es un espacio decorado con elegancia y cuidado. La chimenea proporciona calor en las noches frías, y los sofás y las butacas forman confortables rincones donde disfrutar de unos momentos de descanso.

Il salone è uno spazio arredato con cura ed eleganza. Il camino dà calore nelle fredde notti invernali, mentre i divani e le poltrone formano comodi angoli dove godersi alcuni momenti di relax.

The furniture of this distinguished dining room is elegant and classic in style, and the decorative objects are family heirlooms or holiday souvenirs. The result is a magnificent balance between the sumptuous and the dainty.

Die Möbel in diesem luxuriösen Esszimmer sind elegant und klassisch, und die Dekorationselemente sind persönliche oder Reiseandenken. So entstand ein wundervolles Gleichgewicht zwischen Luxus und Anmut.

Le mobilier de cette salle à manger accueillante est élégant et de style classique, les objets décoratifs sont des souvenirs familiaux ou de voyages. L'ensemble a permis de créer un magnifique équilibre entre somptuosité et délicatesse.

El mobiliario de este distinguido comedor es elegante y de estilo clásico, y los objetos decorativos son recuerdos familiares o de viajes. Con todo ello se ha conseguido un magnífico equilibrio entre suntuosidad y delicadeza.

La mobilia di questa signorile sala da pranzo è elegante e di stile classico, e gli oggetti di arredo sono ricordi di famiglia o di viaggi passati. Grazie a tutto ciò si è riusciti ad ottenere un magnifico equilibrio tra sontuosità e delicatezza.

The bedroom is decorated in a stylish and graceful manner. The canopy bed endows the room with distinction and the remaining features complete the whole picture, with the nightstands, lamps, and chests of drawers recreating an elegant colonial ambience.

Das Schlafzimmer ist anmutig und stilvoll eingerichtet. Das Himmelbett wirkt sehr elegant, und die übrigen Dekorationsobjekte ergänzen die Einrichtung: Nachttische, Lampen und Kommoden schaffen eine elegante, koloniale Atmosphäre.

La chambre est décorée avec grâce et style. Le lit à baldaquin confère sa distinction à la pièce et les autres détails complètent l'ensemble : tables de nuit, lampes et commodes recréent une ambiance coloniale et élégante.

El dormitorio está decorado con gracia y estilo. La cama con dosel otorga distinción a la estancia, y el resto de los detalles completan el conjunto: mesillas de noche, lámparas y cómodas recrean un ambiente colonial y elegante.

La camera da letto è arredata con grazia e stile. Il letto a baldacchino incrementa la signorilità della stanza, a completare l'insieme pensa il resto di oggetti: comodini, lampade e cassettiere che ricreano un ambiente coloniale ed elegante.

House in Barbados

Barbados

Barbados, a small island greatly influenced by the British, has been a luxurious tourist destination for many years thanks to its tropical climate and its Caribbean setting. It is also the location for this magnificent colonial style residence. The architecture combines luminous and elegant interiors with exterior zones which have been designed with exquisite taste, bringing freshness and comfort. All the corners of the residence offer something special, for example, great ocean views can be enjoyed from the first floor porch, and in the bedrooms, the light is filtered through the curtains and creates a delicate and relaxing ambience.

Seit mehreren Jahrzehnten ist Barbados aufgrund seines tropischen Klimas und seiner Lage in der Karibik ein besonders beliebtes Reiseziel. Auf dieser kleinen Insel, die stark von den Briten geprägt wurde, steht dieses wundervolle Haus im Kolonialstil. In seiner Architektur wurden helle und elegante Räume mit Außenbereichen kombiniert, die geschmackvoll gestaltet sind und das Haus frisch und komfortabel machen. Jeder Winkel dieses Hauses ist etwas Besonderes, so kann man zum Beispiel von der Veranda des ersten Stockwerkes aus den Ozean betrachten und in den Schlafzimmern filtert sich das Licht durch die Gardinen und schafft so eine sanfte und entspannende Atmosphäre.

Depuis des décennies, la Barbade est une destination touristique privilégiée grâce à son climat tropical et sa situation dans les Caraïbes. Sur cette petite île – sous grande influence britannique – se trouve cette magnifique résidence de style colonial. L'architecture combine intérieurs lumineux et élégants et zones extérieures pensées avec un goût exquis, offrant fraîcheur et confort. Chaque recoin de la maison est unique : de la véranda au premier étage, il est possible de contempler l'océan, et dans les chambres la lumière filtre à travers les rideaux pour créer une atmosphère délicate et relaxante.

Desde hace varias décadas, Barbados es un destino turístico privilegiado gracias a su clima tropical y a su situación en el Caribe. En esta pequeña isla –de gran influencia británica– se encuentra esta magnífica residencia de estilo colonial. La arquitectura combina unos interiores luminosos y elegantes con unas zonas exteriores diseñadas con un gusto exquisito y que aportan frescura y comodidad. Todos los rincones de la vivienda son especiales: por ejemplo, desde el porche de la primera planta puede contemplarse el océano y en los dormitorios la luz se filtra a través de las cortinas y crea una atmósfera delicada y relajante.

Ormai da tanti anni, Barbados è diventata una meta turistica di prim'ordine grazie al suo clima tropicale e alla sua posizione all'interno dei Caraibi. In questa piccola isola – con una forte influenza britannica – si trova questa magnifica residenza in stile coloniale. L'architettura combina degli interni luminosi ed eleganti con delle zone esterne disegnate con estremo gusto che apportano freschezza e comodità. Tutti gli angoli dell'abitazione hanno qualcosa di speciale: per esempio, dal portico del primo piano si può osservare l'oceano, nelle camere da letto la luce che filtra attraverso le tende crea un'atmosfera delicata e rilassante.

Architect: Morrison Associates
Photographer: © José Luis Hausmann

The island's climate allows for enjoyable exterior zones, which include a small pool and an area for deck chairs. A dining and living area under the porch make for pleasant outdoor living at any time of the day.

Das Klima der Insel macht es möglich, dass man sich oft im Freien aufhalten kann. Deshalb wurde ein kleiner Swimming-pool konstruiert und in einer Ecke steht ein Liegestuhl. Unter der Veranda gibt es eine Essgelegenheit im Freien und einen kleinen Wohnbereich, in dem man sich zu jeder Tageszeit aufhalten kann.

Le climat de l'île permet de jouir des zones extérieures de la maison, dont une petite piscine et un recoin avec chaise-longue. Sous la véranda, une salle à manger et une petite zone de séjour permettent la vie en extérieur à tout moment de la journée.

El clima de la isla permite disfrutar de las zonas exteriores, que incluyen una pequeña piscina y un rincón con una tumbona. Se ha situado bajo el porche un comedor y una pequeña zona de estar para hacer vida en el exterior a cualquier hora del día.

Il clima dell'isola consente di godere delle zona esterne che comprendono una piccola piscina e un angolo con una sdraio. Sotto il portico sono state allestite una zona pranzo e una piccola zona soggiorno dove poter trascorrere piacevoli momenti all'aria aperta in qualsiasi momento della giornata.

House in Garuja

Garuja, São Paulo, Brazil

This simple yet elegant dwelling is located a few meters from the sea and is completely open to the exterior. The lounge and dining area are opened up thanks to some impressive large windows. The breeze and light flow through the windows and inundate modern interiors. Outside, a terrace overlooking the sea, a swimming pool and neat garden create a magnificent environment for moments of relaxation, reading, games and above all, impressive ocean views.

Dieses elegante und gleichzeitig einfache Wohnhaus befindet sich nur wenige Meter vom Meer entfernt und öffnet sich vollständig nach außen. Durch die riesigen Fenster wirken Wohn- und Speisezimmer völlig offen. Die Fenster lassen reichlich Luft und Licht in die Räume strömen. Um das Haus herum liegen die Terrasse zum Meer, der Swimmingpool und der gepflegte Garten, eine wundervolle Umgebung zum Entspannen und Lesen, zum Spielen und vor allem zum Genießen des fantastischen Blicks auf den Ozean.

Élégante et simple, cette maison se trouve à quelques mètres de l'eau et s'ouvre pleinement sur l'extérieur. D'impressionnantes baies vitrées ouvrent complètement la zone du salon et de la salle à manger sur l'extérieur. La brise et la lumière s'infiltrent par les fenêtres et inondent les intérieurs. À l'extérieur, une terrasse face à la mer, une piscine et un jardin bien entretenu forment un cadre magnifique où profiter d'instants de détente ou de lecture, de jeux et, surtout, des vues saisissantes sur l'océan.

Esta elegante y sencilla vivienda se encuentra a escasos metros del mar y toda ella está abierta al exterior. Unos impresionantes ventanales dejan completamente abierta la zona del salón y del comedor. La brisa y la luz entran por las ventanas e inundan las estancias interiores. En el exterior, una terraza frente al mar, una piscina y un cuidado jardín forman un entorno magnífico para disfrutar de momentos de descanso o de lectura, de juegos y, sobretodo, de impactantes vistas al océano.

Sono pochi i metri che separano dal mare questa semplice ma elegante residenza, tutta aperta all'esterno. Grazie a delle grandi vetrate la zona del salone e della sala da pranzo ricevono luce in abbondanza tutto il giorno. La brezza marina e la luce inondano le stanze interne. All'esterno, una terrazza che si affaccia sul mare, una piscina e un giardino ben curato formano un ambiente magnifico dove godersi meritati momenti di relax, un buon libro, giocare spensieratamente, con lo sfondo affascinante dell'oceano.

Architect: Isay Weinfeld
Photographer: © Tuca Reinés

The construction lines create an interesting mix of areas and levels which is heightened by the color white, enhancing the home's shapes. The layout and design of the areas ensure an effect of lightness and luminosity.

Die Linien der Konstruktion lassen ein interessantes Spiel aus Formen und Ebenen entstehen, das von der Farbe Weiß unterstrichen wird. Das Haus wirkt aufgrund der Anordnung und Gestaltung der einzelnen Gebäudeabschnitte leicht und hell.

Les lignes constructionistes de la demeure créent un jeu intéressant de volumes et de niveaux accentué par le blanc qui rehausse ses formes. La disposition et le design des volumes produisent un effet de légèreté et de luminosité.

Las líneas constructivas crean un interesante juego de volúmenes y niveles acentuado por el color blanco, que resalta las formas de la vivienda. La disposición y el diseño de los volúmenes producen un efecto de ligereza y luminosidad.

Le linee costruttive creano un interessante gioco di volumi e di livelli accentuato dal colore bianco che mette in risalto le forme dell'abitazione. La disposizione e il disegno dei volumi producono un effetto di leggerezza e luminosità.

The terraces of this residence are an example of impeccable design and architecture. The small terrace of the upper floor is a vantage point and a simple awning provides shelter from the sun. A wooden deck beside the pool and a garden area of perfect lines create an ideal place to enjoy the sea breeze.

Die Terrassen dieses Wohnhauses sind ein Meisterwerk der Architektur und des Designs. Die kleine Terrasse am Obergeschoss ist eine Aussichtsterrasse aufs Meer mit einem einfachen Sonnendach. Am Swimmingpool bilden eine Holzfläche und ein begrünter Bereich mit perfekten Linien den idealen Ort, um die Meeresbrise zu genießen.

Les terrasses de cette résidence affichent une architecture et un design impeccables. La petite terrasse du niveau supérieur offre un point de vue sur la mer et est dotée d'un auvent simple protégeant du soleil. À côté de la piscine, une superficie de bois et une zone paysagère aux lignes parfaites forment un lieu idéal pour profiter de la brise marine.

Las terrazas de esta residencia muestran una arquitectura y un diseño impecables. La pequeña terraza del piso superior es una atalaya al mar, e incorpora un sencillo toldo que protege del sol. Junto a la piscina, una superficie de madera y una zona ajardinada de líneas perfectas conforman el lugar ideal para disfrutar de la brisa marina.

Le terrazze di questa residenza mostrano un'architettura e un disegno impeccabili. La piccola terrazza del piano superiore sembra una torre di vedetta sul mare, un comodo belvedere protetto dal sole mediante una semplice tenda. Accanto alla piscina, una superficie in legno e una zona verde dai contorni perfetti formano il luogo ideale dove rilassarsi, cullati dal soffio leggero della brezza marina.

Modern House by the Sea

Côte d'Azur, France

The Côte d'Azur is a holiday destination associated with luxury and select ambiences. This exclusive residence has been renovated in order to restore the rooms and to give continuity to the spaces and open them up to the sea. The lower floor houses three different spaces: a study, living room, and modern dining area. The basement which has been completely renewed has a spectacular fitness area and spa. The apparent simplicity of the decoration has touches of audacity, elegance and individuality.

Die Côte d'Azur ist ein Ferienziel, mit dem man Luxus und eine gepflegte Atmosphäre verbindet. Dieses exklusive Haus wurde renoviert, um die Räume zu modernisieren, sie einheitlicher zu machen und zum Meer hin zu öffnen. Im Untergeschoss liegen drei verschiedene Bereiche, ein Atelier, ein Wohnzimmer und ein modern gestaltetes Speisezimmer. Im Kellergeschoss, das auch einer umfassenden Renovierung unterzogen wurde, hat man einen schönen Fitness- und Spa-Bereich geschaffen. Die scheinbare Einfachheit der Dekoration stellt sich bei näherer Betrachtung als ein gewagter, eleganter und sehr persönlicher Stil heraus.

La Côte d'Azur est une destination de vacances associée au luxe et aux atmosphères « select ». Cette résidence exclusive a été repensée pour restaurer les pièces et offrir davantage de continuité aux espaces tout en les ouvrant sur la mer. Le niveau inférieur est constitué de trois espaces différents : une étude, un salon et une salle à manger au design actuel. À la cave, également objet d'une profonde réforme, a été prévue une spectaculaire zone de fitness et de spa. Apparemment simple, la décoration affiche en fait un style audacieux, élégant et personnel.

La Costa Azul es un destino vacacional asociado al lujo y a los ambientes más selectos. Esta exclusiva residencia se ha rehabilitado para restaurar las estancias, dar más continuidad a los espacios y abrirlos al mar. La planta baja contiene tres espacios diferenciados: un estudio, un salón y un comedor de diseño actual. En la planta sótano, objeto también de una profunda remodelación, se ha ubicado una espectacular zona de fitness y spa. La aparente sencillez de la decoración muestra en realidad un estilo audaz, elegante y personal.

La Costa Azzurra è un luogo di villeggiatura legato agli ambienti più raffinati e a un turismo d'elite. I lavori di ristrutturazione di questa residenza hanno avuto come obiettivo quello di dare maggiore continuità agli spazi e di aprirli al mare. Il piano terra è composto da tre spazi differenziati tra loro: uno studio, salone e una sala da pranzo dal design decisamente attuale. Nel piano interrato, anch'esso oggetto di una profonda ristrutturazione, è stata allestita una zona fitness e spa ben attrezzata. L'apparente semplicità dell'arredamento mostra in realtà uno stile audace, ricco di personalità ed eleganza.

Architect: CLS Architetti
Photographer: © Andrea Martiradonna

The terrace is covered in part by lightweight awnings, allowing the enjoyment of exterior spaces and incredible sea views at any time of day. The evenings in this corner of the dwelling can seem to last for ever.

Die Terrasse, die teilweise von leichten Sonnendächern bedeckt ist, ist der ideale Ort, um den Aufenthalt im Freien und den unglaublich schönen Blick aufs Meer zu jeder Tageszeit zu genießen. Die Abenddämmerung in diesem Winkel des Hauses scheint unendlich zu sein.

La terrasse, couverte par endroits de légers auvents, permet de jouir des espaces extérieurs et des incroyables vues sur la mer, à tout moment de la journée. Dans ce recoin de la maison, les crépuscules semblent ne jamais avoir de fin.

La terraza, cubierta en algunas zonas por ligeros toldos, permite disfrutar de los espacios exteriores y de las increíbles vistas al mar a cualquier hora del día. Los atardeceres en este rincón de la vivienda parecen interminables.

La terrazza, coperta in alcuni punti da leggeri tendoni, consente di godere in qualsiasi momento della giornata degli spazi esterni e delle sbalorditive viste sul mare. In quest'angolo dell'abitazione i suggestivi tramonti sembrano non finire mai.

House in Milos

Milos, Greece

This luminous and elegant residence is located on the edge of a 150 feet cliff overlooking the Crete sea. The scattered layout of the structures which make up this house helps bring it into harmony with its surroundings and in doing so protect it from the elements. The house is a contemporary take on the traditional pure white Greek house built using square structures. The bedrooms boast private terraces with spectacular views overlooking the horizon where the sky meets the sea.

Dieses helle und elegante Wohnhaus liegt am Rande einer 50 Meter hohen Steilküste am Meer von Kreta. Die verschiedenen Elemente des Hauses sind über das Grundstück verstreut, so dass es besser in die Landschaft integriert wird und gleichzeitig vor Sonne und Regen geschützt ist. So entsteht eine enge Beziehung zur umgebenden Natur. Das Wohnhaus ist eine moderne Neuinterpretation des traditionellen griechischen Hauses in einem makellosen Weiß und mit quadratischen Formen. An den Schlafzimmern liegen private Terrassen, von denen aus man eine wundervolle Aussicht bis zum Horizont hat und auf denen das Hauptaugenmerk auf Himmel und Meer gerichtet ist.

Lumineuse et élégante, cette résidence se trouve au bord d'une falaise de 50 mètres donnant sur la mer crétoise. La disposition des volumes qui composent la maison, dispersés sur la parcelle pour l'intégrer dans son environnement, permet de la protéger du soleil et de la pluie et de renforcer de la sorte sa relation au paysage. La demeure est une nouvelle interprétation contemporaine de la traditionnelle maison grecque, au blanc immaculé et aux formes carrées. Les chambres disposent de terrasses privées plongeant dans l'horizon et jouissant de vues spectaculaires où le ciel et la mer tiennent la vedette.

Esta luminosa y elegante residencia está situada al borde de un acantilado de 50 metros junto al mar de Creta. La disposición de los volúmenes que componen la vivienda, dispersos por la parcela para integrarla en el entorno, permite protegerla del sol y de la lluvia, y estrechar de este modo su relación con el paisaje. La vivienda es una reinterpretación contemporánea de la casa tradicional griega, de un blanco impoluto y de formas cuadradas. Los dormitorios disponen de terrazas privadas que miran al horizonte y disfrutan de espectaculares vistas, en las que el cielo y el mar son los protagonistas.

Questa luminosa ed elegante residenza è situata ai bordi di una falesia di 50 metri accanto al mare di Creta. La disposizione dei volumi che compongono l'abitazione, sparsi per la parcella per integrarla nell'ambiente circostante, permette di proteggere la casa dal sole e dalla pioggia, e di consolidare in questo modo il suo legame con il paesaggio. L'abitazione è una reinterpretazione contemporanea della casa tradizionale greca, dal bianco immacolato e dalla forme quadrate. Le camere da letto dispongono di terrazzi privati esposti all'orizzonte e da cui si godono viste spettacolari, dove il cielo e il mare sono i veri protagonisti.

Architect: Jean Bocabeille, Ignacio Prego
Photographer: © Ken Hayden / Redcover

The privileged cliff top location make this an exclusive residence. The small windows and thick walls maintain a cool temperature inside, meanwhile the bedroom terraces are perfect for relaxation while enjoying the sea views.

Die wundervolle Lage des Grundstücks über einer Steilküste macht dieses Haus zu etwas ganz Besonderem. Die kleinen Fenster und die dicken Mauern sorgen für Kühle im Inneren, und auf den Terrassen der Schlafzimmer kann man sich mit einem wundervollen Blick aufs Meer entspannen.

L'emplacement privilégié de la maison sur la falaise la convertit en une résidence exclusive. Les petites fenêtres et les murs épais préservent la fraîcheur intérieure alors que les terrasses des chambres offrent un refuge où se reposer tout en profitant des vues sur la mer.

El privilegiado emplazamiento de la casa sobre el acantilado la convierte en una residencia exclusiva. Las pequeñas ventanas y los gruesos muros mantienen una temperatura fresca en el interior, las terrazas de los dormitorios ofrecen un lugar donde descansar mientras se disfruta de las vistas al mar.

La posizione privilegiata sulla falesia rende la casa una residenza esclusiva. Le piccole finestre e gli spessi muri mantengono la temperatura fresca all'interno, mentre i terrazzi delle camere da letto offrono un luogo dove riposare godendo al contempo dell'affascinante veduta del mare.

68   House in Milos *Milos, Greece*

The walkways which link the different structures of the house protect the owners from the unstable climate of the island. The different zones and levels of the house are connected by way of exterior spaces, such as the porch and the concrete staircase. These elements create a dynamic residence which opens out onto its surroundings.

Die Durchgangsbereiche, die die verschiedenen Körper des Hauses miteinander verbinden, sind so geplant, dass die Bewohner vor dem wechselhaften Wetter auf der Insel geschützt sind. Die verschiedenen Zonen und Ebenen des Hauses sind durch Räume im Freien miteinander verbunden, zum Beispiel durch die Veranda und die Betontreppen. Diese Elemente lassen eine dynamische und sich nach außen öffnende Wohnumgebung entstehen.

Des zones de passages ont été disposées afin d'unir les volumes de la demeure pour protéger ses habitants du climat instable de l'île. Les zones et niveaux distincts de la maison sont connectés par des espaces extérieurs, ainsi un porche et des escaliers de béton. Ces éléments créent une résidence dynamique et ouverte sur l'extérieur.

Se han dispuesto las zonas de paso que unen los volúmenes de la vivienda de forma que protejan a sus habitantes del inestable clima de la isla. Las distintas zonas y niveles de la casa están conectados mediante espacios exteriores, como un porche y unas escaleras de hormigón. Estos elementos crean una residencia dinámica y abierta al exterior.

Le zone di passaggio che uniscono i volumi dell'abitazione sono state disposte in maniera da proteggere i loro occupanti dal clima poco stabile dell'isola. Le diverse zone e i livelli della casa sono collegati mediante spazi esterni, quali un portico e delle scale di cemento. Questi elementi creano una residenza dinamica ed aperta all'esterno.

Villa in Capri

Capri, Italy

The island of Capri has been one of the Mediterranean's most famous tourist destinations for more than a century. The residences that were built reflect this luxurious and exclusive ambience which still exists on the island today. This is an antique villa brimming with opulence and elegance. The magnificent sea views can be enjoyed from the porch and from the interiors which evoke times gone by full of history and create a soothing and evocative atmosphere. Past and present are fused together to create a fascinating abode with the antique mural paintings and romantic gardens being some of the influential elements.

Die Insel Capri ist seit über einem Jahrhundert eines der berühmtesten touristischen Ziele im Mittelmeer. Die Häuser, die errichtet wurden, spiegeln diese luxuriöse und exklusive Atmosphäre wider, die auch heute noch auf der Insel herrscht. Hier handelt es sich um eine alte, prachtvolle und elegante Villa. Von der Veranda aus hat man einen wundervollen Blick aufs Meer, und die Räume erinnern an eine ereignisreiche Vergangenheit, so dass eine subtile und phantasieanregende Atmosphäre entsteht. Die Vergangenheit und die Gegenwart bilden eine faszinierende Mischung, in der alte Wandmalereien und die romantischen Gärten zu den wichtigsten Elementen gehören.

Capri est depuis plus d'un siècle l'une des destinations touristiques méditerranéennes les plus prisées. Les résidences construites reflètent l'ambiance de luxe et d'exclusivité qui y perdure. En l'occurrence, une ancienne villa offre son opulence et son élégance. Les magnifiques vues sur la mer offertes par la véranda et les intérieurs remémorant un passé empli d'histoire créent un ensemble évocateur et délicat. Passé et présent se fondent et offrent une vision fascinante où peintures murales anciennes et jardins romantiques ont la vedette.

La isla de Capri es desde hace más de un siglo uno de los destinos turísticos más famosos del Mediterráneo. Las residencias que se construyeron reflejan el ambiente de lujo y exclusividad que aún hoy se vive en la isla. En esta ocasión se muestra una antigua villa llena de opulencia y elegancia. Las magníficas vistas al mar que se disfrutan desde el porche y unos interiores que evocan épocas pasadas llenas de historia crean un conjunto evocador y delicado. Pasado y presente se funden para proporcionar una visión fascinante en la que antiguas pinturas murales y románticos jardines son algunos de sus protagonistas.

Da tempo ormai l'isola di Capri è una delle mete turistiche più famose del Mediterraneo. Le ville costruite nell'isola rispecchiano l'ambiente raffinato ed esclusivo che ancora oggi si respira. In questa occasione si mostra un'antica villa piena di opulenza ed eleganza. Gli interni, molto delicati e suggestivi, evocano epoche passate, piene di storia; dal portico si gode una vista magnifica che arriva fino al mare. Passato e presente si fondono in questa dimora dove tra le varie attrattive spiccano antichi dipinti murari e dei romantici giardini curati alla perfezione.

Interior design: Vicky de Dalmases de Romano
Photographer: © Ricardo Labougle

One of the terrace areas is covered to provide welcome respite from the sun. The decoration gives the space an atmosphere reminiscent of Arabian tents, which makes for a special corner where the tranquil summer nights can be enjoyed.

Ein Teil der Terrasse wurde überdacht, um ihn vor der Sonne zu schützen. Die Dekoration erinnert an Nomadenzelte, ein ganz besonderer Ort, um die Sommernächte zu genießen.

L'une des parties de la terrasse a été couverte pour assurer un espace ombragé. La décoration donne à l'espace une atmosphère rappelant les jaimas arabes et transforme ce recoin unique où profiter des paisibles nuits estivales.

Una de las áreas de la terraza se ha cubierto para proporcionar un espacio de sombra. La decoración concede al espacio una atmósfera que recuerda las jaimas árabes y que se convierte en un rincón especial donde disfrutar de las noches de verano.

Una delle zone della terrazza è stata coperta per creare uno spazio d'ombra. L'arredamento crea la tipica atmosfera di una jaima araba; un ambiente suggestivo ed accogliente dove trascorrere una piacevole serata estiva.

The vegetation is an important element of this porch. The flowers and creeping plants create a nostalgic and romantic space. Some comfortable wicker chairs and an iron table with ceramic tiles bring freshness to the ambience and become the perfect accessories for an exterior space.

Die Vegetation ist ein sehr wichtiges Element auf dieser Veranda. Blumen und Kletterpflanzen machen die Umgebung romantisch und nostalgisch. Komfortable Korbsessel und ein schmiedeeiserner Tisch mit Keramikkacheln sorgen für Frische und bilden die perfekte Ergänzung dieses Platzes im Freien.

La végétation est un élément très important de cette véranda. Les fleurs et les plantes grimpantes créent un espace romantique et nostalgique. De confortables fauteuils en osier et une table de fer forgé recouverte de céramique apportent fraîcheur à l'atmosphère et complémentent parfaitement l'espace extérieur.

La vegetación es un elemento muy importante en este porche. Las flores y las plantas enredaderas crean un espacio romántico y nostálgico. Unos confortables sillones de estructura de mimbre y una mesa de forja con azulejos de cerámica aportan frescura al ambiente y se convierten en el complemento perfecto para un espacio exterior.

La vegetazione è un elemento molto importante in questo portico. I fiori e le piante rampicanti creano uno spazio romantico e al contempo nostalgico. Lo spazio esterno viene completato da comode poltrone di vimini e da una tavola in ferro battuto con piastrelle smaltate.

The main living room of this villa is a majestic and extremely elegant room. The very high ceilings with the mural paintings bring distinction to the space. The careful choice of the curtains and the upholstery accentuate the richness of the details.

Der Hauptsalon dieser Villa ist ein herrschaftlicher und besonders eleganter Raum. Die sehr hohen Decken und die Wandmalereien machen ihn sehr edel. Auch die sorgfältig ausgewählten Gardinen und Polster unterstreichen die edle Atmosphäre.

Le salon principal de cette villa est un lieu majestueux et extrêmement élégant. Les plafonds surélevés et couverts de peintures murales apportent sa distinction à l'espace. Les tentures et tapisseries, choisies judicieusement, accentuent la richesse des détails.

El salón principal de esta villa es un lugar majestuoso y extremadamente elegante. Unos techos altísimos con pinturas murales aportan distinción al espacio. Las cortinas y las tapicerías, escogidas con gran acierto, acentúan la riqueza de los detalles.

Il salone principale di questa villa è una stanza maestosa ed estremamente elegante. Dei soffitti altissimi con dei pregevoli affreschi alle pareti donano distinzione a tutto l'ambiente. I tendaggi e la tappezzeria, accuratamente scelti, accentuano la raffinatezza dei dettagli decorativi.

Positano Villa

Positano, Italy

The objective of the alterations to this fantastic Italian residence, once part of a monastery, was the creation of a contemporary space within a historic context. The interpretation of traditional architecture has resulted in a majestic interior where the great height of the living room and original 18th and 19th century ceramic features are highlights. The main bedroom also contains ceramic features. Outside there is a small Arabian-inspired pool and an elegant terrace with breathtaking sea views.

Bei der Umgestaltung dieses wundervollen Hauses in Italien, das einst Teil eines Klosters war, wollte man eine moderne Wohnung innerhalb eines historischen Kontexts schaffen. Durch die Neuinterpretation der traditionellen Architektur entstanden herrschaftliche Räume, in denen vor allem das Wohnzimmer durch seine Höhe und die Originalkeramik aus dem 18. und 19. Jh. auffällt. Im Hauptschlafzimmer wurde die gleiche Keramik verwendet. Am Haus befinden sich ein kleiner Swimmingpool im arabischen Stil und eine hübsche Terrasse mit einem schönen Blick aufs Meer.

L'intervention de l'architecte dans cette fantastique résidence italienne, qui formait partie d'un monastère, à été pensée afin de créer un espace contemporain dans un cadre historique. La ré-interpretation de l'architecture traditionelle résulte en un interieur majestueux. La hauteur des plafonds et la céramique originale des XVIIIème et XIXème siècles retiennent particulièrement l'attention. On retrouve aussi ce type de céramique dans la chambre principale. L'extérieur nous présente une petite piscine aux réminiscences arabes et une terrasse délicate aux vues imprenables sur la mer.

La intervención en esta fantástica residencia italiana, que formó parte de un monasterio, se realizó con idea de crear un espacio contemporáneo dentro de un contexto histórico. La interpretación de la arquitectura tradicional ha dado como resultado un majestuoso interior, donde destaca la gran altura del salón y la cerámica original de los siglos XVIII y XIX. En el dormitorio principal también encontramos este tipo de cerámica. En el exterior se encuentra una pequeña piscina de reminiscencias árabes y una delicada terraza con impactantes vistas al mar.

L'intervento eseguito in questa fantastica villa italiana, che faceva parte di un vecchio monastero, è stato realizzato con l'idea di creare uno spazio contemporaneo all'interno di un contesto storico. L'interpretazione delle tradizioni architettoniche ha dato come risultato degli interni maestosi, dove spicca la grande altezza del salone e la ceramica originale del XVIII e XIX secolo. Questo tipo di ceramica si trova anche nella camera da letto principal. All'esterno si trova una piccola piscina di reminescenze arabe e una suggestiva terrazza con magnifiche viste sul mare.

Architect: Lazzarini Pickering Architetti
Photographer: © Matteo Piazza

The terrace has been designed in a simplistic manner, although the sea views and elegant lines create a graceful and subtle effect. Here the main attraction is the subtlety of the shapes which accentuate the natural setting.

Die Terrasse ist scheinbar sehr einfach gestaltet, aber der Blick aufs Meer und die eleganten Linien machen diesen Ort sehr anmutig und elegant. Die Terrasse ist durch die subtilen Formen, die die umgebende Natur unterstreichen, ganz besonders schön.

La terrasse est un espace pensé avec une simplicité apparente, mais les vues sur la mer et l'élégance de ses lignes donnent grâce et délicatesse à l'espace. L'attrait principal de ce lieu réside dans la subtilité des formes qui se distinguent savamment du cadre naturel.

La terraza es un espacio diseñado aparentemente con sencillez, pero las vistas al mar y la elegancia de sus líneas otorgan al espacio una gran gracia y delicadeza. Éste es un lugar en el que el atractivo principal reside en la sutileza de las formas que consiguen destacar el entorno natural.

La terrazza è uno spazio disegnato con apparente semplicità, ma le viste sul mare e l'eleganza delle linee la trasformano in uno spazio dotato di grazia e delicatezza. Il fascino principale del luogo risiede nelle forme leggere che mettono in risalto la natura circostante.

The terrace has been designed in a simplistic manner, although the sea views and elegant lines create a graceful and subtle effect. Here the main attraction is the subtlety of the shapes which accentuate the natural setting.

Die Terrasse ist scheinbar sehr einfach gestaltet, aber der Blick aufs Meer und die eleganten Linien machen diesen Ort sehr anmutig und elegant. Die Terrasse ist durch die subtilen Formen, die die umgebende Natur unterstreichen, ganz besonders schön.

Equis House

Cañete, Peru

This residence is a key example in showing how architecture can meld itself perfectly with a natural setting. In this case the setting is a spectacular enclave on the coast where a balanced and environmentally friendly design has been used. The house is a solid yet elegant structure with spaces that link the interior with the exterior. The house looks out onto the horizon and the spacious exterior terrace resembles a beach which stretches down to the ocean and houses a long narrow transparent swimming pool. The straight lines and ochre colors give the house serenity and prestige.

Dieses Haus ist ein Beispiel dafür, wie sich die Architektur perfekt in eine natürliche Umgebung, in diesem Fall ein wundervoller Ort an der Küste, integrieren kann, und zwar durch eine sorgfältige Planung, die respektvoll mit der Umwelt umgeht. Das Haus ist ein eleganter und solider Körper mit Räumen, die außen und innen miteinander verbinden. Es steht direkt am Meer mit Blick auf den Horizont, und die große Terrasse wirkt wie ein Strand, der über einen langen, schmalen Swimmingpool mit transparentem Wasser bis zum Ozean reicht. Die geraden Linien und Ockertöne lassen das Haus schlicht und edel wirken.

Cette résidence est un exemple de la manière dont l'architecture peut parfaitement s'intégrer dans le cadre naturel – une enclave spectaculaire face à la côte – grâce à un design équilibré et respectueux du milieu l'accueillant. La maison forme un volume élégant et solide dont les espaces assurent la relation entre l'intérieur et l'extérieur. Ancrée face à la mer, la demeure tourne le regard vers l'horizon et la vaste terrasse extérieure est comme une plage qui s'étend vers l'océan à travers une piscine transparente, longue et étroite. De la sorte, les lignes droites et l'ocre des couleurs confèrent à l'endroit sérénité et prestance.

Esta residencia es un ejemplo de cómo la arquitectura puede integrarse perfectamente en el entorno natural –un espectacular enclave frente a la costa– gracias a un diseño equilibrado y respetuoso con el medio ambiente. La casa forma un volumen elegante y sólido, con espacios que relacionan el interior con el exterior. Anclada frente al mar, la casa mira hacia el horizonte y la amplia terraza exterior es como una playa que se extiende hacia el océano a través de una piscina transparente, larga y estrecha. Asimismo, las líneas rectas y los colores ocres otorgan a la vivienda serenidad y prestancia.

Questa residenza è un esempio di come l'architettura possa integrarsi perfettamente nell'ambiente naturale – un luogo spettacolare di fronte alla costa – grazie ad un disegno equilibrato e rispettoso nei confronti dell'ambiente stesso. La casa forma un volume elegante e solido, con spazi che mettono in comunicazione l'interno con l'esterno. Ancorata di fronte al mare, la casa guarda verso l'orizzonte e l'ampia terrazza esterna è come una spiaggia che si prolunga fino all'oceano attraverso una piscina trasparente lunga e stretta. Le linee rette e i colori ocra conferiscono all'edificio serenità e prestanza.

Architect: Barclay & Crousse
Photographer: © Barclay & Crousse

Sobriety and elegance define the style of this residence both in the exterior architecture and in the interior design where nature and the ocean take center stage. The residence serves as an ideal summer retreat, somewhere to relax and pamper oneself.

Der Stil dieses Hauses ist einfach und elegant, das betrifft sowohl die Anlage der Außenbereiche als auch die Innenarchitektur. Die Hauptrolle in dieser Wohnumgebung spielen stets die Natur und das Meer. So wird das Haus zu einem idealen Zufluchtsort für den Sommer, ein Ort, an dem man sich entspannen und sich seiner selbst widmen kann.

Sobriété et élégance définissent le style de la demeure, tant pour l'architecture extérieure que pour la décoration intérieure, et abandonnent le devant de la scène à la nature et à l'océan. De ce fait, la maison devient un refuge idéal pour profiter de l'été, un lieu où se reposer et se consacrer à soi même.

Sobriedad y elegancia definen el estilo de esta vivienda, tanto en la arquitectura exterior como en la decoración interior, y ceden todo el protagonismo a la naturaleza y al océano. De este modo, la vivienda se convierte en un refugio ideal para disfrutar del verano, un lugar donde descansar y dedicarse a uno mismo.

Sobrietà ed eleganza definiscono lo stile di questa abitazione, sia per quanto riguarda l'architettura esterna che per l'arredamento degli interni; a farla da protagonisti sono invece la natura e l'oceano. In questo modo l'abitazione si trasforma in un rifugio ideale dove godersi l'estate, in un luogo dove rilassarsi e dedicarsi ai propri hobby.

Vistas of Simplicity

Cape Town, South Africa

This dwelling has been designed with a view to creating a close link between inside and outside. The materials and the design of the spaces have been carefully used to create cohesion between the outdoor landscape and the indoor rooms of the house. From the porch and the pool the magnificent views over the bay can be enjoyed. The bedroom and bathroom are very elegant and comfortable rooms and their simplicity creates a calm and relaxing atmosphere. The living room, decorated following the same color scheme, is an ideal place for a quite read or rest.

Bei der Gestaltung dieses Hauses wollte man eine enge Beziehung zwischen innen und außen schaffen. Die benutzten Materialien und die Raumgestaltung trugen zu diesem Zusammenfließen der äußeren Landschaft mit den Räumen des Hauses bei. Von der Veranda und dem Swimmingpool aus hat man einen wunderschönen Blick auf die Bucht. Das Schlafzimmer und das Bad sind komfortabel und elegant gestaltet, und auch hier entsteht durch Schlichtheit viel Ruhe und Gelassenheit. Das Wohnzimmer ist mit den gleichen Farben dekoriert, es lädt zur Lektüre und zum Ausruhen ein.

Le design de cette demeure à été réalisé avec l'intention de lier étroitement intérieur et extérieur. Les matériaux et le concept spatial ont généré la cohésion entre le paysage extérieur et les pièces de la maison. Depuis la véranda et la piscine, de magnifiques vues sur la baie s'offrent à la contemplation. La chambre et la salle de bains sont deux pièces confortables et élégantes dont la simplicité permet également de jouir d'une ambiance détendue et apaisée. Le salon, dans les mêmes tonalités, est le lieu idéal pour apprécier la lecture et le repos.

El diseño de los espacios de esta vivienda y los materiales muestran una estrecha relación entre el paisaje exterior y las estancias interiores de la casa. Desde el porche y la piscina se puede disfrutar de unas magníficas vistas a la bahía. El dormitorio y el baño son dos estancias muy confortables y elegantes, cuya sencillez también permite gozar de una atmósfera relajante y calmada. El salón, decorado con la misma gama de colores, es un lugar idóneo para disfrutar de la lectura y del descanso.

Il disegno architettonico e i materiali di questa residenza evidenziano la stretta coesione tra l'interno e l'esterno. Dal portico e la piscina si godono magnifiche viste della baia. La camera da letto e il bagno sono stanze confortevoli ed eleganti, dove regna la semplicità e la tranquillità. Il salone, che presenta la stessa gamma di colori, è il luogo ideale per una piacevole lettura o per semplici momenti di relax.

Interior design: Faline Edwards
Photographer: © Craig Fraser / Redcover.com

The exterior space of the dwelling is perfect for enjoying the impressive views of the natural landscapes which surround the house. The extraordinary location allows for enjoyment of the mountains, the ocean and ultimately gives the residence exclusivity and appeal.

Von den Außenbereichen des Hauses aus hat man einen sehr schönen Blick auf die umgebende Natur. An diesem einzigartigen Standort kann man sowohl die Berge als auch das Meer genießen, eine sehr exklusive und beeindruckende Lage.

L'espace extérieur de la demeure incite à se griser des vues saisissantes de la nature dont la maison est entourée. Son emplacement extraordinaire permet de profiter de la montagne et de l'océan tout en assurant exclusivité et séduction à la résidence.

El espacio exterior de la vivienda permite gozar de unas impactantes vistas a la naturaleza que rodea la casa: la extraordinaria ubicación permite disfrutar de la montaña y el océano y proporciona a la residencia exclusividad y atractivo.

L'esterno della residenza permette di godere di impressionanti viste alla natura che circonda la casa; le montagne e l'oceano ne fanno un luogo esclusivo e affascinante.

The living room is an elegant space which opens out onto the exterior. The materials used for the sofas and cushions transform the interior into a delicate and extremely comfortable room. The inflowing light creates a truly peaceful and serene atmosphere.

Das Wohnzimmer ist elegant gestaltet und öffnet sich nach draußen. Die Stoffe, mit denen die Sofas und Kissen überzogen sind, machen den Raum sehr elegant und komfortabel. Durch das Tageslicht, das in die Räume fällt, entsteht eine friedliche und gelassene Atmosphäre.

Le salon est une pièce élégante et ouverte sur l'extérieur. Les toiles revêtant sofas et coussins transforment cet intérieur en un lieu délicat et confortable au plus haut degré. La lumière qui pénêtre à l'intérieur procure une incroyable atmosphère de paix et de sérénité.

El salón es una estancia elegante y abierta al exterior. Las telas que visten los sofás y cojines transforman el interior en una estancia delicada y extremadamente confortable. La luz que penetra en el interior proporciona una increíble atmósfera de paz y serenidad.

Il salone, arredato con eleganza e buon gusto, si apre all'esterno. Le stoffe dei divani e dei cuscini danno all'ambiente degli interni un tocco di delicata raffinatezza e di esclusivo comfort. La luce che penetra inonda di pace e tranquillità tutta la stanza.

Seascapes
Umkomaas, South Africa

This original residence situated on the South African coast exhibits a rustic air. Wood has been used practically throughout the entire house bringing comfort and warmth. Thoughtful decoration has added to the delicate and harmonious ambience. The color white and the varying textures of the curtains and upholsteries create an evanescent, luminous and almost magical atmosphere. Outside, the porch, a magnificent terrace and a swimming pool constitute a perfect space where the youngest members of the family can play and enjoy the fresh air.

Dieses originelle Haus an der südafrikanischen Küste wirkt sehr ländlich. Fast am ganzen Haus wurde Holz verwendet, was es sehr komfortabel und warm wirken lässt. Durch die liebevolle Dekoration wurde eine feine und harmonische Atmosphäre geschaffen, die Farbe Weiß und die verschiedenen Texturen der Gardinen und Polster schaffen eine leichte, helle, fast magische Atmosphäre. Draußen befinden sich eine Veranda, eine wundervolle Terrasse und ein Swimmingpool, hier können die Kinder der Familie in einer wundervollen Umgebung im Freien spielen.

Cette résidence originale, située face à la côte sud-africaine, se caractérise par ses airs rustiques. Le bois a été employé dans presque toute la maison, apportant une sensation de confort et de chaleur. Un minutieux travail de décoration a permis de créer une ambiance délicate et harmonieuse : le blanc et les différentes textures des tentures et tapisseries créent une atmosphère evanescente, lumineuse, presque magique. À l'extérieur, la véranda, la magnifique terrasse et la piscine forment un espace parfait pour que les plus jeunes de la famille puissent jouer à l'air libre.

Esta original residencia situada frente a la costa sudafricana se caracteriza por un aire rústico. Se ha empleado la madera en prácticamente toda la casa, lo que aporta sensación de confort y calidez. Esto ha sido posible gracias a un minucioso trabajo de decoración para conseguir un ambiente delicado y armonioso; el blanco y las diferentes texturas de cortinas y tapicerías crean una atmósfera evanescente, luminosa y casi mágica. En el exterior, un porche, una magnífica terraza y la piscina conforman un espacio perfecto para que los más jóvenes de la familia puedan jugar al aire libre.

Questa originale residenza sita di fronte alla costa sudafricana si caratterizza per il suo aspetto rustico. Il legno è stato adoperato praticamente in tutta la casa, aumentando così la sensazione di comfort e accoglienza. A questo ha indubbiamente contribuito un minuzioso arredamento volto ad ottenere un ambiente delicato ed armonioso; il bianco e le diverse texture di tende e tappezzerie creano un'atmosfera evanescente, luminosa e quasi magica. All'esterno, un portico, una magnifica terrazza e la piscina danno vita a uno spazio ideale dove i più giovani della famiglia possono giocare liberamente all'aria aperta.

Architect: Pennington &Associates
Photographers: © T. Chance / H&L / Inside / Cover

The living room is a simple space, where the diversity of upholsteries creates an original and elegant atmosphere. The remaining furniture highlights the rustic style which characterizes the decoration of the house.

Das Speisezimmer ist ein einfacher Raum, in dem die verschiedenen Stoffe eine elegante und originelle Atmosphäre schaffen. Die übrigen Möbel unterstreichen den rustikalen Stil, der die Dekoration dieses Hauses kennzeichnet.

La salle à manger est un espace simple où la diversité des tapisseries crée une atmosphère élégante et coloniale. Le reste du mobilier souligne le style rustique qui caractérise la décoration de la maison.

El comedor es un espacio sencillo, donde la diversidad de tapizados crean una atmósfera elegante y original. El resto del mobiliario subraya el estilo rústico que caracteriza la decoración de la casa.

La sala da pranzo è uno spazio semplice, dove la varietà di stoffe e tessuti crea un'atmosfera elegante ed originale. Il resto dei mobili sottolinea lo stile rustico che caratterizza l'arredamento della casa.

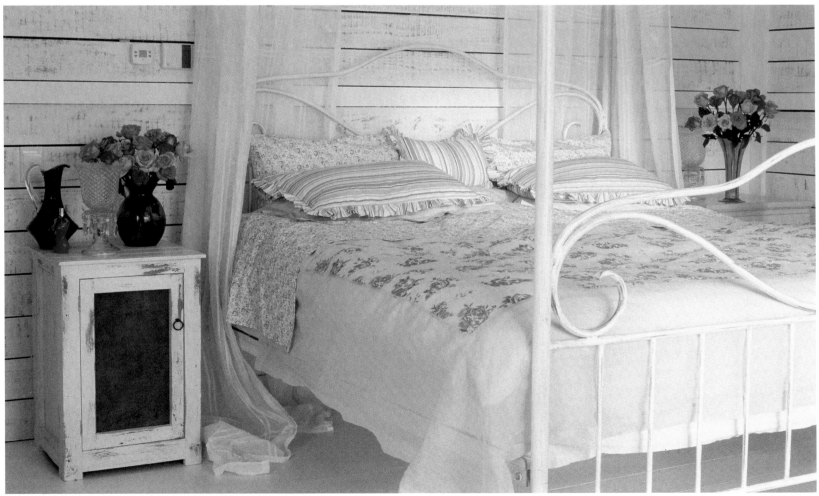

Can Km 15

Ibiza, Spain

Ibiza is renowned for its beauty and for being a valued tourist destination. This residence captures perfectly the image of modernity and style which this idyllic island portrays. The lines of the architecture are extremely clean and give lightness and elegance to the construction. Interior courtyards with vegetation, where water and stone are central elements, create a charming space. The interiors are original and somber, giving class and appeal to a dwelling which thanks to its shapes and magnificent exterior views is truly captivating.

Die Insel Ibiza ist für ihre wundervolle Landschaft bekannt und dafür, dass sie ein so beliebtes Reiseziel ist. Dieses Haus ist ein perfektes Beispiel für die Modernität und den Stil, den man auf dieser idyllischen Insel findet. Die architektonischen Linien sind besonders rein und lassen das Gebäude leicht und elegant wirken. Die begrünten Innenhöfe, deren wichtigste Elemente Wasser und Stein sind, schaffen eine bezaubernde Atmosphäre. Die originellen und natürlich gestalteten Räume machen das Haus stilvoll und anziehend. Hinzu kommen die interessanten Formen und der wundervolle Ausblick.

Ibiza est un endroit connu pour la beauté de ses paysages et pour être l'une des destinations touristiques les plus prisées au monde. La résidence ici présentée s'ajuste à la perfection à l'image de modernité et de style communiquée par cette île idyllique. Les lignes de l'architecture sont extrêmement limpides et confèrent légèreté et élégance à la construction. Des patios intérieurs dont les éléments principiaux sont l'eau et la pierre sont peuplés de végétation créant des espaces enchanteurs. Les intérieurs, originaux et sobres, offrent classe et séduction à une demeure qui captive par ses formes et ses magnifiques vues sur l'extérieur.

Ibiza es un lugar conocido por sus bellos parajes y por ser uno de los destinos turísticos más valorados. La residencia que se muestra a continuación se ajusta a la perfección a la imagen de modernidad y estilo que desprende esta idílica isla. Las líneas de la arquitectura son extremadamente limpias y confieren ligereza y elegancia a la construcción. Unos patios interiores con vegetación, cuyos elementos principales son el agua y la piedra, crean un espacio lleno de encanto. Los interiores, originales y sobrios, otorgan clase y atractivo a una vivienda que cautiva por sus formas y por sus magníficas vistas al exterior.

Ibiza non è solo una delle mete turistiche più gettonate tra i giovani, ma anche un'isola nota per le sue bellezze naturali. Paesaggi a dir poco idilliaci fanno da sfondo a case, ville che tra lo stile moderno ed il tradizionale, si inseriscono senza stonature nel tessuto urbano ibicenco. Le linee architettoniche di questa villa sono estremamente semplici, pure, e donano leggerezza ed eleganza all'edificio. Alcuni cortili interni ricchi di fiori e piante, dove l'acqua e la pietra sono gli elementi principali, danno vita a uno spazio incantevole, ideale per rilassarsi. Gli interni, originali e sobri, donano classe e fascino a un'abitazione che colpisce per le sue forme e per le magnifiche vedute panoramiche.

Architect: Bruno Erpicum
Photographer: © Jean Luc Laloux

The pool has extremely pure and clean lines. White predominates in the exterior decoration and brings calmness to the ambience. Two elegant chairs facing the sea have been placed under the canopy.

Der Swimmingpool zeigt sich in besonders reinen und klaren Linien. Im Freien herrscht die Farbe Weiß vor, die eine ruhige und friedliche Stimmung entstehen lässt. Unter der Markise stehen zwei elegante Sessel, von denen aus man aufs Meer schaut.

Les lignes de la piscine sont extrêmement pures et limpides. Le blanc qui prédomine les extérieurs anime l'ambiance d'une atmosphère emplie de sérénité. Sous la marquise, deux élégants fauteuils ont été prévus, orientés vers la mer.

La piscina tiene unas líneas extremadamente puras y limpias. El color blanco que predomina en los exteriores le otorga al ambiente una atmósfera llena de calma. Bajo la marquesina se han situado dos elegantes sillones orientados hacia el mar.

La piscina presenta delle linee estremamente sobrie. Il bianco, colore che predomina all'esterno, crea un'atmosfera piena di calma. Sotto la tettoia sono state sistemate due eleganti poltrone orientate verso il mare.

The interior of this dwelling has a contemporary style. The quality of the materials, the works of art and the chosen color schemes, result in elegant rooms with class.

Das Haus ist sehr modern eingerichtet. Die hochwertigen Materialien, die Kunstwerke und die gelungenen Farbkombinationen lassen stilvolle und elegante Räume entstehen.

L'intérieur de cette demeure présente un style contemporain marqué. Les pièces élégantes et stylées résultent de la qualité des matériaux, des œuvres d'art et du choix judicieux des couleurs.

El interior de esta vivienda tiene un marcado estilo contemporáneo, sobrio y sencillo. La calidad de los materiales, las obras de arte y la acertada elección de los colores dan como resultado unas estancias elegantes y con clase.

Gli interni di questa abitazione hanno un marcato stile contemporaneo. La qualità dei materiali, le opere d'arte e l'accurata scelta dei colori danno come risultato degli ambienti eleganti dotati di classe.

Can Labacaho

Ibiza, Spain

This dwelling is situated at the top of a slight hill, above the traditional terraces used in agriculture, enjoying great views over the Mediterranean Sea. The house is composed of three different areas. The main area, made of cement, stands out for its great presence. The second area, made of glass, is open towards the south and creates a separate exterior space through a piece of furniture designed by the architect. The third area, in between the two previous areas, is made of wood. The works of contemporary art which decorate the whole dwelling bring an air of distinction and style; an outdoor pool completes the whole effect.

Dieses Haus liegt auf einem sanften Hügel auf Terrassen, wie sie für die Landwirtschaft angelegt werden, und es bietet einen schönen Blick auf das Mittelmeer. Das Haus besteht aus drei Teilen, der Hauptteil aus Beton ist besonders auffällig, der zweite Teil ist verglast und nach Süden hin offen, so dass ein Raum im Freien entstand, der durch Möbel abgetrennt wird, die der Architekt selbst entworfen hat. Der dritte Teil des Hauses, der zwischen den beiden anderen liegt, ist aus Holz. Das Haus ist mit Werken zeitgenössischer Kunst dekoriert, die es edel und stilvoll wirken lassen. Ein Swimmingpool im Freien vervollständigt das Gesamtbild.

Cette maison est située au sommet d'une colline aux pentes douces et aux terrasses traditionnellement cultivées, et permet de jouir de vues sur la Méditerranée. Elle est composée de trois volumes principaux : le principal, en béton, à beaucoup de présence ; le second, vitré, est ouvert sur le sud, c'est un espace extérieur séparé par le mobilier spécialement conçu par l'architecte ; le troisième, entre les deux, est tout de bois vêtu. Les œuvres d'art contemporain décorant la maison lui confèrent distinction et style ; une piscine extérieure complète l'ensemble.

Esta casa está situada en lo alto de una suave colina, sobre las tradicionales terrazas de uso agrícola, y permite disfrutar de vistas al mar Mediterráneo. Se compone de tres volúmenes: el principal, de hormigón, destaca por su gran presencia; el segundo, acristalado, está abierto hacia el sur y crea un espacio exterior separado mediante mobiliario que ha diseñado el arquitecto, y el tercero, entre los dos anteriores, está realizado con madera. Las obras de arte contemporáneo que decoran la vivienda le otorgan distinción y estilo; una piscina exterior completa el conjunto.

Questa casa è situata in cima a una lieve collina, sui tradizionali terrazzi agricoli, con magnifiche vedute del mar Mediterraneo. Si compone di tre volumi: il principale, di cemento, spicca per la sua grande presenza; il secondo, tutto in vetro, si apre verso sud e crea una spazio esterno separato mediante dei mobili disegnati dall'architetto, e il terzo, sito tra i due volumi precedenti, è realizzato in legno. Le varie opere d'arte che decorano l'abitazione le conferiscono distinzione e stile; una piscina esterna completa l'insieme.

Architect: Bruno Erpicum
Photographer: © Jean Luc Laloux

The pool, situated on the west wing, harmonizes with the extremely clean lines of the architecture. An interior courtyard with high walls painted in a daring violet, separates the master bedroom from the other areas of the house.

Der Swimmingpool am Westflügel passt ausgezeichnet zu der Architektur mit ihren extrem klaren Linien. Die hohen Wände des Innenhofes sind in einem gewagten Violett gestrichen. Dieser Hof trennt das Hauptschlafzimmer von den übrigen Räumen des Hauses.

La piscine, située à l'aile ouest, s'harmonise avec l'architecture aux lignes extrêmement limpides. Un patio intérieur aux parois élevées et peintes d'un violet audacieux sépare la chambre principale des autres parties de la maison.

La piscina, situada en el ala oeste, armoniza con la arquitectura de líneas extremadamente limpias. Un patio interior, con paredes de gran altura pintadas de un atrevido color violeta, separa el dormitorio principal de las demás áreas de la casa.

La piscina, situata nell'ala ovest della casa, è in perfetta armonia con l'ambiente circostante e le linee architettoniche dell'edificio. Un patio interno, con pareti molto alte dipinte di un audace violetto, separa la camera da letto principale dalle altre aree della casa.

The raised location of the dwelling heightens the enjoyment of the spectacular views of the town and sea. The elegant lines of construction give an air of distinction to the house and a pond at one side of the house creates a relaxing space from where to enjoy the landscapes.

Durch die erhöhte Lage des Hauses hat man einen überwältigenden Blick auf das Dorf und das Meer. Die eleganten Linien lassen das Haus sehr edel wirken. An einem der Flügel des Gebäudes liegt ein Teich, der eine friedvolle Umgebung entstehen lässt, in der man die Landschaft genießen kann.

La situation élevée de la demeure permet de profiter de vues spectaculaires sur le village et la mer. Les lignes élégantes de la construction confèrent sa distinction à la maison. Un étang situé à côté de l'une des ailes de la résidence crée un espace de détente depuis lequel profiter du paysage.

La elevada ubicación de la vivienda permite disfrutar de unas espectaculares vistas a la población y al mar. Las elegantes líneas de la construcción otorgan distinción a la casa. Un estanque situado junto a una de las alas de la casa crea un espacio relajante desde donde disfrutar del paisaje.

L'elevata posizione della dimora consente di godere di spettacolari viste sul mare e sull'intera località. Le eleganti linee architettoniche donano distinzione a tutto l'edificio. Un laghetto situato accanto ad una delle ali della casa crea uno spazio rilassante dove godersi tranquillamente l'affascinante paesaggio dei dintorni.

118   Can Labacaho *Ibiza, Spain*

The living room is located in a clear, open space, which also contains the kitchen and indoor dining area. The spaces have different styles due to the furniture arrangements, including unique pieces designed by the same architect, Bruno Erpicum. The result is an interior of great elegance and incomparable style.

Das Wohnzimmer liegt innerhalb eines klar gegliederten Raumes, in dem sich auch die Küche und das im Haus gelegene Speisezimmer befinden. Die einzelnen Bereiche werden durch die Anordnung und die Möbel, die der Architekt Bruno Erpicum selbst entworfen hat, unterschieden. Das Ergebnis ist ein sehr eleganter und stilvoller Raum.

Le salon se place dans l'espace ouvert qui accueille également la cuisine et la salle à manger intérieure. Les espaces se définissent grâce à la distribution du mobilier- toutes des créations uniques créées par Bruno Erpicum, l'architecte. Il en résulte un espace de grande élégance et au style incomparable.

El salón se ubica dentro de un espacio diáfano, en el que también se encuentran la cocina y el comedor interior. Los espacios se diferencian gracias a la distribución y al mobiliario, piezas singulares diseñadas por el mismo arquitecto, Bruno Erpicum. El resultado es un espacio de gran elegancia y de un estilo incomparable.

Il salone si trova in uno spazio diafano, nel quale trovano posto anche la cucina e la sala da pranzo interna. Gli spazi vengono differenziati grazie alla distribuzione e alla mobilia, composta da pezzi singolari disegnati dallo stesso architetto, Bruno Erpicum. Nel complesso, ne risulta uno spazio di grande eleganza e dallo stile incomparabile.

House in Ibiza

Ibiza, Spain

Situated on the side of a mountain and with views of the Mediterranean, this residence is made up of two houses, the main dwelling and one for guests. The design is elegant, and unostentatious while the pure lines enhance the architecture. The area where the pool is located connects the two houses and holds a large terrace with incredible sea views. The house is surrounded by woods and the exterior porch areas. The rectangular shapes, straight lines and light colors result in an architecture of open structures.

Dieses Haus an einem Berghang und mit Blick auf das Mittelmeer besteht eigentlich aus zwei Häusern, dem Wohnhaus der Eigentümer und dem Gästehaus. Es ist sehr elegant gestaltet, jedoch ohne Übertreibungen, und die reinen Linien unterstreichen die Architektur. Der Swimmingpool, neben dem eine große Terrasse mit einem unglaublich schönen Blick aufs Meer liegt, verbindet die beiden Häuser. Das Haus ist von Veranden umgeben und von Bäumen, die es schützen. Die rechteckigen Formen, die geraden Linien und die hellen Farben schaffen eine Architektur mit offenen Strukturen.

Située à flanc de montagne avec vue sur la Méditerranée, cette résidence se compose de deux maisons, la demeure principale et celle des invités. Sans ostentation, le design est élégant et les lignes épurées rehaussent la qualité de l'architecture. La zone accueillant la piscine connecte les deux maisons et comprend une vaste terrasse avec d'incroyables vues sur la mer. Entourée de zones extérieures, comme par exemple les vérandas, la maison est protégée par une aire boisée. Les volumes rectangulaires, les lignes droites et les tons clairs soulignent une architecture aux structures ouvertes.

Situada en la ladera de una montaña y con vistas al mediterráneo, esta residencia se compone de dos casas, la vivienda principal y la de los invitados. Sin ostentaciones, el diseño es elegante y sus líneas depuradas resaltan su arquitectura. El área donde se encuentra la piscina conecta las dos casas e incorpora una amplia terraza con unas increíbles vistas al mar. Rodeada de otras zonas exteriores, como los porches, la casa está protegida por una zona boscosa. Los volúmenes rectangulares, las líneas rectas y los tonos claros crean una arquitectura de estructuras abiertas.

Adagiata sul fianco di una montagna e con vedute al mar Mediterraneo, questa residenza è composta da due case: l'abitazione principale e quella degli ospiti. Privo di sfarzi, il disegno è elegante e le sue linee sobrie risaltano l'architettura dell'edificio. L'area dove si trova la piscina collega le due case e ingloba un'ampia terrazza con delle magnifiche viste sul mare. Circondata da altre zone esterne, come i portici, la casa è protetta da una zona boscosa. I volumi rettangolari, le linee rette e i toni chiari creano un insieme architettonico di strutture aperte.

Architect: Juan de los Ríos
Photographer: © Lourdes Grivé

The elegant deck chairs positioned alongside the infinity pool, the living area with outdoor furniture and the surrounding vegetation melt together to bring an elegant aesthetic and almost minimalist feel to the house.

Die eleganten Liegestühle an dem schönen „Infinity"-Pool, der Wohnbereich im Freien mit den hübschen Gartenmöbeln und die Vegetation, die das Grundstück umgibt, machen das Haus elegant und fast minimalistisch.

Les élégantes chaises longues disposées au bord de la piscine de style « infini », la zone de séjour avec son mobilier d'extérieur et la végétation ceignant le lieu confèrent à cette demeure une esthétique élégante quasi minimaliste.

Las elegantes tumbonas dispuestas junto a una piscina desbordante, la zona de estar con mobiliario de exteriores y la vegetación que rodea la finca confieren a la vivienda una estética elegante y casi minimalista.

Le eleganti sdraio disposte accanto alla piscina senza bordi, la zona soggiorno con i tipici mobili da giardino e la vegetazione che circonda la tenuta conferiscono all'abitazione un'estetica elegante e quasi minimalista.

Stone walls protect the house, create the layout of the flowerbeds and also help to delimit the different levels, forming spaces where the local vegetation can grow. Within the property, walls of the same material highlight the boundaries of each building.

Das Haus wird von Natursteinmauern geschützt, die die Anordnung von Terrassenfeldern ermöglichen und die verschiedenen Ebenen begrenzen, auf denen einheimische Pflanzen wachsen. Im Inneren bestehen die Mauern aus dem gleichen Material und begrenzen die einzelnen Gebäudeteile.

Des murs de pierre protègent la maison, recréant la disposition de certains étagements et délimitant différents niveaux, dont ces espaces où laisser pousser la végétation locale. À l'intérieur de la propriété, de petits murets construits du même matériau marquent les limites des volumes.

Unos muros de piedra protegen la casa, recrean la disposición de unos bancales y delimitan los diferentes niveles formando espacios donde dejar crecer la vegetación autóctona. En el interior de la finca, pequeños muros construidos con mismo material marcan los límites de los volúmenes.

Alcuni muri di pietra proteggono la casa, ricreano la disposizione a terrazzamenti e delimitano i vari livelli formando spazi dove far crescere la vegetazione autoctona. All'interno della tenuta, dei piccoli muri costruiti con lo stesso materiale segnano i limiti dei volumi.

Inside this house, levels were introduced to allow the architecture to adapt to the land and assume vitality and dynamism. The furniture, light floors and white walls create a contemporary style interior.

Im Inneren dieses Hauses hat man verschiedene Ebenen geschaffen, um es an die Höhenunterschiede des Geländes anzupassen. Dadurch wirkt es sehr lebendig und dynamisch. Die Möbel und die hellen Bodenfliesen in Kombination mit den weißen Wänden und den Dekorationselementen schaffen ein modernes Interieur.

À l'intérieur de cette demeure naît un jeu entre les niveaux qui permet à l'architecture de s'adapter au terrain, tout en lui conférant vitalité et dynamisme. Le mobilier, le revêtement du sol aux tons clairs accompagnant le blanc des murs et les éléments décoratifs créent un intérieur au style contemporain.

En el interior se ha diseñado un juego de niveles para adaptar la arquitectura al terreno y darle vitalidad y dinamismo. El mobiliario, el pavimento y las paredes, de tonos claros, junto con los elementos decorativos, crean un interior de estilo contemporáneo.

All'interno è stato creato un gioco di livelli che fa sì che l'architettura si adatti al terreno ed acquisisca vitalità e dinamismo. La mobilia, il pavimento e le pareti, dai toni chiari, insieme agli elementi di arredo, creano degli interni di stile contemporaneo.

Small Refuge in Mallorca

Mallorca, Spain

This small house is owned by an art and antiques dealer. Close to the town of Palma, this idyllic place has been transformed into a haven to escape from the daily stresses of life. The dwelling is simplistic and stands out because of its Mediterranean inspired delicate decoration. In the interior, a central oriental theme is apparent in the oil lamps, rugs and throws which all add to the colorful and relaxed atmosphere. The relaxation area next to a small cove of transparent water is another privileged corner of this property, a real hide out and sanctuary of peace.

Dieses kleine Haus gehört einem Kunst- und Antiquitätenhändler. Es liegt in der Nähe von Palma in einer sehr idyllischen Umgebung, in der man sich gut von dem täglichen Arbeitsstress erholen kann. Das Haus ist sehr einfach gestaltet und mit viel Sorgfalt im mediterranen Stil dekoriert. Im Inneren besteht die Dekoration aus vielen orientalischen Objekten wie Öllampen, Teppichen und Bettüberwürfen, die eine entspannte und sehr farbenfrohe Atmosphäre schaffen. Die Ruhezone an der kleinen Bucht mit kristallklarem Wasser ist ein weiterer, besonders schöner Winkel dieses Hauses, ein Versteck, in dem man Ruhe und Frieden findet.

Cette petite maison appartient à un marchand d'art et d'antiquités. À proximité de Palma, ce site idyllique se convertit en un refuge où déconnecter du stress du travail quotidien. La simple demeure se distingue par une décoration d'une grande délicatesse, aux airs méditerranéens. À l'intérieur on note une foule d'objets orientaux ainsi que des lampes à huile, des tapis et couvre-lits, qui contribuent à créer une ambiance détendue et colorée. La zone de repos, juste à côté de la petite crique aux eaux limpides, est l'un des autres recoins de cette propriété : une véritable cachette où trouver la paix.

Esta pequeña casa es propiedad de un marchante de arte y antigüedades. Cercano a la ciudad de Palma, este idílico lugar se convierte en un refugio donde desconectar del estrés del trabajo diario. La vivienda es sencilla y destaca por una decoración de gran delicadeza y de aire mediterráneo. En el interior destacan multitud de objetos orientales, como lámparas de aceite, alfombras y cubrecamas, que contribuyen a crear un ambiente relajado y colorista. La zona de descanso junto a la pequeña cala de aguas transparentes es otro de los privilegiados rincones de esta propiedad, un verdadero escondite en el que encontrar la paz.

Questa piccola residenza è proprietà di un mercante d'arte e di oggetti di antiquariato. Questo luogo idillico, non molto distante dalla città di Palma, diventa un tranquillo rifugio dove staccare dalla routine quotidiana. Pur nella sua semplicità, l'abitazione spicca per l'arredamento delicato e tipicamente mediterraneo. Negli interni trovano posto svariati oggetti di arredo in stile orientale quali lampade ad olio, tappeti e copriletto, i cui peculiari colori danno vita all'atmosfera rilassante di questo ambiente. Nei pressi di una piccola ed appartata cala dalle acqua cristalline si trova la zona relax, un altro angolo privilegiato di questa dimora, un vero nascondiglio dove trovare pace e tranquillità.

Architect: Toni Muntaner
Photographer: © Andreas von Einsiedel

The house is situated next to one of the numerous coves on the island. The vegetation is characterized by autochthonous pine trees and cacti. The Arabian inspired rugs and cushions create a true Mediterranean ambience.

Das Haus liegt an einer der zahlreichen Buchten der Insel. Die umgebende Vegetation besteht aus den für die Region typischen Pinien und Kakteen. Die Räume sind voller arabischer Teppiche und Kissen und wirken sehr mediterran.

La maison est proche de l'une des nombreuses criques qui entourent l'île. La végétation se caractérise par des pins et des cactus typiques de la région. La décoration des lieux, fourmillant de tapis et coussins à l'esthétique arabe, crée une ambiance résolument méditerranéenne.

La casa se encuentra junto a una de las numerosas calas que bordean la isla. La vegetación se caracteriza por los pinos y cactus típicos de la región. La decoración del lugar, lleno de alfombras y cojines de estética árabe, crea un ambiente absolutamente mediterráneo.

La casa si trova accanto a una delle numerose cale che punteggiano il litorale maiorchino. La vegetazione dei dintorni è tipicamente mediterranea, caratterizzata da pini e cactus. L'arredamento degli interni viene ravvivato dai colori dei vari tappeti e cuscini di estetica araba sparsi per le stanze della casa.

134   Small Refuge in Mallorca *Mallorca, Spain*

The terrace with spectacular views of the Mediterranean Sea is one of the most luxurious spaces of the dwelling. It is a great spot for enjoying the sunsets and dinners al fresco. The only items of furniture are an iron and mosaic table and some wicker chairs, protected by a simple canvas awning which provides welcome shelter from the sun.

Die Terrasse mit dem wundervollen Blick aufs Mittelmeer ist einer der luxuriösesten Bereiche des Hauses. Hier kann man die wundervolle Abenddämmerung und fantastische Abendessen unter freiem Himmel genießen. Die einzigen Möbel auf dieser Terrasse sind der schmiedeeiserne Tisch mit Mosaiken und ein paar Korbstühle. Ein einfaches Sonnendach aus Leinen spendet wohltuenden Schatten.

La terrasse aux vues spectaculaires sur la Méditerranée est l'un des endroits les plus luxueux de la demeure. Il est possible d'y apprécier de délicieux crépuscules et de fantastiques dîners en plain air. Une table de fer forgé couverte de mosaïques et quelques chaises en osier en constituent le seul mobilier. Un simple auvent en toile, protégeant du soleil, complète l'ensemble.

La terraza con espectaculares vistas al mar Mediterráneo es uno de los lugares más lujosos de la vivienda. En ella se puede disfrutar de deliciosos atardeceres y fantásticas cenas al aire libre. Los únicos muebles que la componen son una mesa de forja y mosaico y unas sillas de mimbre. Un sencillo toldo de lona que protege del sol completa el conjunto.

La terrazza con spettacolari vedute sul mar Mediterraneo è uno degli angoli più suggestivi dell'abitazione. Il luogo ideale dove ammirare gli tramonti estivi e organizzare cene all'aria aperta. Gli unici mobili che la compongono sono un tavolo in ferro battuto e mosaico e alcune sedie di vimini. L'insieme viene completato da un tendone d'olona che ripara la terrazza dai raggi del sole.

Paradise in the Caribbean

St. Lucia

This magnificent villa situated on an island in the heart of the Caribbean is the ideal place to relax and enjoy holiday time. The year long pleasant climate and the beauty of its surroundings make for true paradise. Its colonial style, both inside and out, breathes calmness and serenity. Comfortable teak furniture fills the luminous living room and the white and blue colors lend elegance and simplicity to the dwelling. The bedrooms boast balconies with amazing sea views. Outside, a summer house serves as a charming place for intimate dinners.

Diese wundervolle Villa auf einer Insel mitten in der Karibik ist der perfekte Ort zum Ausruhen und für die Ferien. Hier herrscht das ganze Jahr über ein sehr angenehmes Klima, und eine unglaublich schöne Natur umgibt das Haus. Das Haus ist sowohl innen als auch außen im Kolonialstil gehalten, der Ruhe und Gelassenheit ausstrahlt. Komfortable Möbel aus Teakholz statten das helle Wohnzimmer aus und die Farben Weiß und Blau lassen die Wohnung schlicht und elegant wirken. An den Schlafzimmern befindet sich ein Balkon, von dem aus man einen überwältigenden Blick auf das Meer hat. Ein kleines Gartenhäuschen ist der ideale Ort für romantische und intime Abendessen.

Cette magnifique villa située sur une île au cœur des Caraïbes est le lieu idéal pour se reposer et jouir de la saison estivale. Ici, il devient possible de profiter toute l'année d'un climat agréable et du cadre paradisiaque. De style colonial, l'intérieur comme l'extérieur inspirent calme et sérénité. De confortables meubles en teck décorent le salon lumineux et les tons blancs et bleus inondent la demeure de simplicité et d'élégance. Les chambres comptent un balcon offrant des vues saisissantes sur la mer. À l'extérieur, une gloriette se convertit en un refuge enchanteur pour célébrer des repas intimes.

Esta magnífica villa situada en una isla en medio del Caribe es el lugar perfecto para descansar y disfrutar de la temporada de vacaciones. En ella se puede disfrutar durante todo el año de un agradable clima y de un entorno paradisíaco. De estilo colonial, tanto el interior como el exterior se respira calma y serenidad. Confortables muebles de teca decoran el luminoso salón, y los colores blanco y azul inundan la vivienda con sencillez y elegancia. Los dormitorios cuentan con un balcón desde el que disfrutar de impactantes vistas al mar. En el exterior, una glorieta se convierte en un encantador refugio para celebrar cenas íntimas.

Questa magnifica villa situata su un'isola in mezzo ai Caraibi è il luogo perfetto dove riposare e godersi un piacevole soggiorno in villeggiatura. Il clima mite e la natura circostante ne fanno un angolo paradisiaco. Il suo stile è coloniale, e sia all'interno che all'esterno si respira calma e tranquillità. Confortevoli mobili in legno di tek abbelliscono il luminoso salone; i colori predominanti dell'abitazione, il bianco e il blu, conferiscono all'insieme semplicità ed eleganza. Le camere da letto sono dotate di un pratico balcone da cui affacciarsi e godere le fantastiche vedute sul mare. All'esterno, un gazebo diventa in incantevole rifugio dove celebrare cene intime.

Interior design: Piers and Astrid Ashbourne
Photographer: © Andreas von Einsiedel

The setting for this residence is one of its greatest assets. The proximity of the ocean, the luxuriant vegetation and the impressive views all help to create a truly idyllic dwelling.

Die wundervolle Natur der Umgebung verleiht diesem Haus einen besonderenzauber. Es liegt in der Nähe des Meeres, ist von üppiger Vegetation umgeben und man hat einen überwältigenden Blick auf den Ozean, der das Haus einfach perfekt macht.

L'environnement accueillant de cette résidence constitue l'un de ses attraits majeurs. La proximité de l'océan, la végétation luxuriante et ses vues impressionnantes lui confèrent une valeur ajoutée.

El entorno en el que se ubica esta residencia constituye uno de sus mayores atractivos. La proximidad del océano, la frondosa vegetación y las impresionantes vistas le otorgan un valor añadido.

L'attrattiva di questa residenza è il luogo in cui si trova. La prossimità dell'oceano, la vegetazione lussureggiante e le magnifiche viste conferiscono alla residenza un elevato valore aggiunto.

The porch is one of the most luxurious places of the dwelling thanks to its strategic location and use of materials and space. The colonial style architecture and decoration create a space brimming with charm. The rattan furniture provides a pleasant outdoor living room where long conversations can linger on into the night.

Die Veranda ist aufgrund ihrer günstigen Lage, der verwendeten Materialien und der Anordnung der verschiedenen Elemente einer der elegantesten Bereiche des Hauses. Die koloniale Architektur und Dekoration schaffen eine faszinierende Umgebung. Die Rattanmöbel lassen dieses Wohnzimmer im Freien sehr freundlich wirken, es lädt zu langen nächtlichen Unterhaltungen im Freien ein.

Le véranda est l'un des lieux les plus élégants de la maison, de par son emplacement stratégique, les matériaux employés et la disposition des différents éléments. L'architecture et la décoration de style colonial créent un espace plain d'enchantement. Les meubles en rotin apportent leur chaleur à ce salon extérieur qui permet de profiter de longues conversations au coucher du soleil.

El porche es uno de los lugares más elegantes de la vivienda, por su estratégica ubicación, por los materiales que emplea y por la disposición de los diferentes elementos. La arquitectura y la decoración colonial crean un espacio lleno de encanto. Los muebles de ratán aportan calidez a este salón exterior que permite disfrutar de largas conversaciones al anochecer.

Il portico è uno dei luoghi più eleganti dell'abitazione, per la sua posizione strategica, per i materiali adoperati e per la disposizione dei diversi elementi. L'architettura e l'arredamento coloniale creano uno spazio pieno di fascino. I mobili in ratan apportano calore a questo salone esterno che consente di intrattenersi in lunghe conversazioni fino al calar del sole.

A sinuous swimming pool and some comfortable deck chairs make for the perfect space for having a relaxing dip. The pleasant climate and sun can be fully enjoyed in the exterior zones, such as the porch, the terrace and the swimming pool, without loss of privacy.

Der geschwungene Swimmingpool und die komfortablen Liegestühle sind die perfekte Umgebung für ein erfrischendes Bad. In den Außenbereichen wie auf der Veranda, der Terrasse und am Swimmingpool kann man die Sonne und das angenehme Klima genießen, ohne auf die Intimsphäre verzichten zu müssen.

Une piscine sinueuse et les chaises longues confortables constituent l'espace parfait pour se submerger dans un bain de plaisir. Les zones extérieures, comme la véranda, la terrasse et la piscine, permettent de jouir du soleil et du climat agréable sans perdre l'intimité assurée par cette demeure particulière.

Una sinuosa piscina y unas confortables tumbonas conforman el espacio perfecto para sumergirse en un placentero baño. Las zonas exteriores, como el porche, la terraza y la piscina, permiten disfrutar del sol y del agradable clima sin perder la privacidad que proporciona una finca particular.

Una piscina dalle forme sinuose e delle comode sdraio formano lo spazio ideale per un tuffo rinfrescante all'aria aperta. Le zone esterne, come il portico, la terrazza e la piscina, consentono di godere del sole e del clima sempre mite nell'assoluta privacy di una villa privata.

Residence in St. Lucia

St. Lucia

This residence situated on an island in the Caribbean Sea is an example of the fusion of simplicity and luxury. A calm and peaceful ambience has been attained. The excellent finishes, the purity of lines, the colors and small decorative features achieve a harmonious whole and transform it into the perfect residence for retirement and rest. Some features like the roof and the wooden beams or the traditional chimney give the space a rural touch. The marvelous sea views can be enjoyed from a small terrace and also from the walkway surrounding the house.

Dieses Haus auf einer Insel in der Karibik ist ein ausgezeichnetes Beispiel für Schlichtheit und Luxus. Die Atmosphäre strahlt Ruhe und Gelassenheit aus. Die edlen Oberflächenmaterialien, die reinen Linien und Farben und die kleinen Dekorationselemente schaffen ein harmonisches Ganzes und machen das Haus zu einem idealen Ort des Rückzugs und der Erholung. Einige der Elemente wie das Dach, die Holzbalken und der traditionelle Kamin lassen es ein wenig ländlich wirken. Ein Durchgangsbereich, von dem aus man den Blick genießen kann, umgibt das Haus. Von einer kleinen Terrasse aus hat man einen wundervollen Blick aufs Meer.

Cette résidence située sur l'une des îles de la mer des Caraïbes est aussi un exemple de simplicité et de luxe. L'ambiance est calme et sereine. Finitions parfaites, pureté des lignes et des couleurs, petits détails décoratifs… tout se conjugue en un ensemble harmonieux et fait de cette résidence un lieu parfait pour la retraite et le repos. Quelques éléments, tels que la couverte et les poutres de bois, ou encore la cheminée traditionnelle, lui donnent une touche rurale. Une zone de passage entoure la demeure et permet d'en contempler l'extérieur. Depuis une petite terrasse, on goûte de merveilleuses vues sur la mer.

Esta vivienda situada en una isla del mar del Caribe es, al mismo tiempo, un ejemplo de sencillez y lujo. Se ha conseguido un ambiente calmado y sosegado; los excelentes acabados, la pureza de las líneas y de los colores y los pequeños detalles decorativos consiguen un armonioso conjunto y transforman esta residencia en un lugar perfecto para el retiro y el descanso. Algunos elementos, como la cubierta y las vigas de madera o la chimenea tradicional, le proporcionan un toque rural. Una zona de paso rodea la casa y permite contemplar el exterior. Desde una pequeña terraza se disfrutan también de unas maravillosas vistas al mar.

Questa dimora, situata in un'isola del Mar dei Caraibi è un esempio di semplicità e al tempo stesso di eleganza. Per via della sua ubicazione, l'ambiente che vi si respira è di assoluta tranquillità. Le eccellenti rifiniture, la purezza delle linee e dei colori e i piccoli dettagli decorativi riescono a dar vita ad un armonioso complesso, perfetto per rilassarsi e riposarsi. Alcuni elementi, come la copertura e le travi in legno o il camino tradizionale danno all'insieme un tocco rustico. La casa è circondata da una zona di passaggio che permette di osservare meglio tutto l'esterno. Da una piccola terrazza si possono ammirare splendide viste panoramiche sul mare.

Architect: Ian Morrison
Interior design: Judy and Mark Johnson
Photographer: © Andreas von Einsiedel

The lounge has been decorated very carefully. White brings lightness and helps increase the luminosity of the house. The use of wood brings warmth to the interior. The island's warm climate has resulted in an absence of some of the exterior walls.

Bei der Gestaltung des Wohnzimmers achtete man auch auf das kleinste Detail. Die Farbe Weiß lässt das Haus geräumig und hell wirken, und das Holz, ein Element, das hier besonders auffällt, macht die Atmosphäre warm und freundlich. Um das angenehme Klima der Insel wirklich auszunutzen, verzichtete man auf einige Außenwände, so dass das Haus nicht vollständig geschlossen ist.

Le salon est une pièce à laquelle on a porté une attention soignée jusque dans le moindre détail. Le blanc apporte de la légèreté et contribue à éxacerber la luminosité de la maison, et le bois, l'un des matériaux vedette, apporte une atmosphère chaleureuse. Afin de tirer parti du climat de l'île, certaines parois extérieures ont été « oubliées », de sorte que la pièce n'est pas complètement fermée.

El salón es una estancia en la que se ha cuidado hasta el mínimo detalle. El blanco aporta ligereza y contribuye a potenciar la luminosidad de la casa, y la madera, uno de los materiales más destacados, otorga calidez al ambiente. Para aprovechar el agradable clima de la isla, se ha prescindido de algunas paredes exteriores, de modo que la estancia no queda totalmente cerrada.

Il salone è una delle stanze che è stata arredata minuziosamente prestando attenzione ad ogni particolare. La leggerezza del bianco si sposa mirabilmente con la luminosità che pervade tutta la casa. A dare una nota di calore a tutto l'ambiente è il legno, uno dei principali materiali utilizzati. Al fine di poter sfruttare al massimo il clima temperato di quest'isola caraibica, si è deciso di eliminare alcune pareti esterne.

Sterzin House

Fire Island, USA

This residence, situated on an island where driving is prohibited, is surrounded by vegetation. The impressive scenery, the proximity of the sea and the peace and tranquility all add to the enjoyment. The exterior architecture evokes a simple, almost austere sea front retreat, although the interiors are decorated in a warm classic style brimming with decorative details such as photographs, candles, vases and fresh flowers. These elements endow the house with comfort and warmth. Some marine inspired features are also part of the decoration of this house which to sum up is a distinguished and elegant sea front dwelling.

Dieses Haus steht auf einer Insel, auf der keine Autos fahren dürfen, und es ist von der einheimischen Vegetation umgeben. Die beeindruckende Landschaft, die Nähe des Meeres und die Ruhe machen diesen Standort ganz besonders schön. Von außen wirkt das Gebäude eher wie eine einfache, fast karge Hütte am Meer, aber die Räume sind in einem klassischen und ansprechenden Stil dekoriert, voller liebevoller Details wie Fotografien, Kerzen, Krüge und Gestecke voller frischer Blumen. Diese Elemente und die Dekorationsstücke, die an das Meer erinnern, machen das Haus sehr einladend und komfortabel. Ein elegantes und edles Haus direkt am Meer.

Cette résidence, située sur une île où la circulation automobile est prohibée, est entourée de végétation. Le paysage saisissant, la proximité de la mer et la tranquillité qui se respirent sont une valeur ajoutée de ce lieu. L'architecture extérieure évoque un refuge simple et quasi austère au bord de la mer, bien qu'à l'intérieur la décoration soit classique et chaleureuse, avec profusion de détails tels que photographies, bougies, et vases de fleurs fraîches. Ces éléments confèrent chaleur et confort à la maison, qui compte aussi quelques motifs marins. Il s'agit tout simplement d'une demeure élégante et distinguée au bord de la mer.

Esta residencia, situada en una isla donde está prohibida la circulación de coches, se encuentra rodeada de vegetación. El impactante paisaje, la proximidad del mar y la tranquilidad que se respira aportan un valor añadido. La arquitectura exterior evoca un sencillo y casi austero refugio junto al mar, aunque en su interior la decoración es clásica y cálida, con profusión de detalles como fotografías, velas, jarrones y centros repletos de flores frescas. Estos elementos otorgan calidez y confort a la casa, que también cuenta con algunos motivos marineros. Sencillamente, se trata de una elegante y distinguida vivienda junto al mar.

Questa dimora, circondata da una lussureggiante vegetazione, sorge su un'isola in cui è vietato il transito alle auto. Il paesaggio, a dir poco, la vicinanza del mare e la tranquillità che si respira apportano un notevole valore aggiunto. L'architettura esterna evoca un semplice e quasi austero rifugio accanto al mare, sebbene l'arredamento degli interni sia di tipo classico, con toni caldi, profusione di dettagli come fotografie, candele, vasi e centrotavola pieni di fiori freschi. Questi elementi conferiscono calore e comfort alla casa, che sfoggia anche alcuni motivi marinari. Si tratta semplicemente di un'elegante e distinta abitazione accanto al mare.

Architect: Donald Sterzin
Photographer: © T. Jeanson / Inside / Cover

The ambience pervading this house is elegant and romantic. Flowers and plants are present in every corner of the living room and an Ionic column accentuates the classicism of the decoration and brings a regal touch to the room.

In diesem Haus herrscht eine elegante und romantische Atmosphäre, in allen Winkeln des Wohnzimmers stehen Blumen und Pflanzen, und eine ionische Säule unterstreicht die klassische Dekoration und lässt den Raum majestätisch wirken.

L'ambiance de la maison est élégante et romantique : les fleurs et les plantes envahissent chaque recoin du salon et une colonne ionique accentue le classicisme de la décoration tout en offrant sa majesté à la pièce.

El ambiente que se respira en la casa es elegante y romántico; las flores y las plantas invaden todos los rincones del salón y una columna jónica acentúa el clasicismo de la decoración y aporta majestuosidad a la estancia.

L'ambiente che si respira nella casa è elegante e romantico; i fiori e le piante invadono tutti gli angoli del salone e una colonna ionica accentua il classicismo dell'arredamento, conferendo al tempo stesso sontuosità alla stanza.

Interiors are brought to life through detail; in this residence, the orchids, candles and small decorative objects create a warm and cozy ambience.

Dieses Haus verdankt seine Persönlichkeit vor allem den kleinen, liebevollen Details wie den Orchideen, den Kerzen und kleinen Dekorationsobjekten, die eine warme und freundliche Atmosphäre schaffen.

Ce sont les petites nuances qui donnent leur personnalité aux intérieurs : dans cette résidence, orchidées, bougies et petits objets décoratifs créent une ambiance accueillante et chaleureuse.

Los pequeños matices son los que aportan personalidad a los interiores; en esta residencia, las orquídeas, las velas y los pequeños objetos decorativos crean un ambiente acogedor y cálido.

Sono i piccoli dettagli e le sfumature che danno personalità agli interni; in questa residenza, le orchidee, le candele e i piccoli oggetti di arredo creano un ambiente gradevole e accogliente.

An extensive collection of black and white photographs of Native North Americans and fashion shots by Horst P. Horst and Herbert List are displayed on one of the walls of this room.

Eine umfassende Sammlung von Schwarz-Weiß-Fotografien von nordamerikanischen Indianern und Modeaufnahmen von Horst P. Horst und Herbert List hängen an einer der Wände des Raumes.

Une vaste collection de photographies en noir et blanc d'indiens nord-américains et d'images de mode de Horst P. Horst et de Herbert List est concentrée sur l'un des murs de la pièce.

Una extensa colección de fotografías en blanco y negro de nativos norteamericanos e imágenes de moda de Horst P. Horst y Herbert List se concentran en una de las paredes de la estancia.

Una vasta collezione di fotografie in bianco e nero di nativi nordamericani e alcune immagini di moda di Horst P. Horst e Herbert List si concentrano in una delle pareti della stanza.

Dunbar Residence

Maui, USA

Built on top of volcanic rock, this residence on the west coast of Maui is surrounded by lush vegetation and the waters of the Pacific. The interior enjoys magnificent views of the three reefs which protect the house, and the ground floor houses an enormous living room with a large 10 foot high window opening out onto the terrace. Outside there is an infinity swimming pool, partly covered by a projecting roof—one of the most significant elements of the construction—, which produces a visual effect of the water extending to the horizon.

Dieses Wohnhaus an der Westküste von Maui befindet sich auf Vulkangestein und ist von üppiger Vegetation und dem Wasser des Pazifik umgeben. Vom Inneren aus genießt man einen wundervollen Blick auf die drei Riffs, die das Haus beschützen. Im Erdgeschoss liegt ein großes Wohnzimmer mit einem riesigen, über drei Meter hohen Fenster zur Terrasse. Auf dieser befindet sich der „Infinity-Swimmingpool", der teilweise von einem Dachvorsprung überdacht ist und sich bis ins Meer zu verlängern scheint. Der Dachvorsprung ist das auffallendste Konstruktionsmerkmal des Hauses.

Assise sur une roche volcanique, cette résidence de la côte ouest de Maui est cernée par une végétation omniprésente et les eaux du Pacifique. L'intérieur jouit de panoramas magnifiques sur les trois récifs qui protègent la maison. Le niveau principal abrite une salle de séjour énorme proposant une grande baie vitrée de plus de trois mètres s'ouvrant sur la terrasse. Celle-ci accueille une piscine « infinity » partiellement occultée par une couverte en porte-à-faux, l'un des éléments les plus significatifs de la construction, qui semble s'étendre jusqu'à la mer.

Asentada sobre roca volcánica, esta residencia de la costa oeste de Maui se halla rodeada por una abundante vegetación y por las aguas del Pacífico. El interior disfruta de magníficas panorámicas de los tres arrecifes que protegen la casa y el piso principal alberga una enorme sala de estar con una gran ventana de más de tres metros que se abre a la terraza. En ella se encuentra una piscina "infinity" parcialmente tapada por una cubierta en voladizo –uno de los elementos más significativos de la construcción–, que parece prolongarse hasta el mar.

Arroccata su un'altura di roccia vulcanica, questa residenza della costa ovest di Maui è circondata da una fitta vegetazione e dalle acque dell'oceano Pacifico. Dall'interno è possibile godere della magnifica vista panoramica delle tre scogliere che proteggono la casa; il piano principale accoglie un enorme soggiorno con una grande finestra lunga più di tre metri che si apre sulla terrazza. Qui trova posto una piscina "infinity", parzialmente coperta da un tetto in aggetto – uno degli elementi di spicco dell'edificio –, che sembra prolungarsi fino al mare.

Architect: Nick Milkovich, Arthur Erickson
Photographer: © Ron Dahlquist, Tim Street-Porter

A large sized window joins the living room to the terrace and slides completely open. This allows for great views of the waves breaking on the rocks from the terrace and even from inside the lounge.

Ein riesiges Fenster, das fast zu verschwinden scheint, vereint das Wohnzimmer mit der Terrasse. So sieht man von der Terrasse und vom Wohnzimmer aus, wie die Wellen gegen die Felsen schlagen.

Une grande baie vitrée unit la salle de séjour et la terrasse et glisse pour presque disparaître. De la sorte, il devient loisible de contempler les vagues se briser sur les rochers depuis la terrasse, voire l'intérieur du salon.

Un gran ventanal une la sala de estar y la terraza y se desliza hasta casi desaparecer. De este modo, desde la terraza y desde el interior del salón se pueden ver las olas rompiendo contra las rocas.

Una grande vetrata unisce il soggiorno e la terrazza e si fonde con l'esterno fino quasi a scomparire. In questo modo, si possono osservare le onde che si infrangono nelle rocce sia dalla terrazza che dall'interno del salone.

Miami Beach 50's

Miami, USA

This magnificent house was built in 1938, as an extension of an existing house. The present day owners transformed it into their first residence after alterations to adapt it to the local climate. Outside there is a fantastic pool, a porch complete with cozy dining area, some designer hammocks and a private quay giving direct access to the sea. The interior is brimming with style. The choice of colors and furniture makes for a distinguished and modern ambience.

Dieses wundervolle Haus wurde 1938 als Erweiterung eines bereits existierenden Gebäudes geschaffen. Die augenblicklichen Besitzer haben es zu ihrem ständigen Wohnsitz umgebaut und dabei an das Klima der Region angepasst. Das Haus besitzt einen ganz bezaubernden Swimmingpool, eine Veranda, die als Speisezimmer im Freien dient, und elegante Liegestühle. Außerdem kann man von einem privaten Landesteg aus direkt hinaus aufs Meer. Die Räume sind sehr stilvoll gestaltet, durch die Auswahl der Farben und der Möbel wurde ein moderner und edler Wohnbereich geschaffen.

Cette magnifique maison a été construite en 1938, en complément d'une autre déjà existante. Les propriétaires actuels en ont fait leur résidence habituelle après les travaux de réforme visant à l'adapter au climat local. L'extérieur présente une piscine fantastique, une véranda et une salle à manger accueillante aux hamacs design. De plus, un ponton privé offre un accès direct à la mer. L'intérieur affirme son style : le choix des couleurs et du mobilier assure une ambiance moderne et distinguée.

Esta magnífica casa fue construida en 1938 como ampliación de una ya existente. Los actuales propietarios la transformaron en su residencia habitual tras una reforma para adaptarla al clima de la zona. En el exterior se encuentra una fantástica piscina, un porche con un acogedor comedor y unas hamacas de diseño. Además, un muelle privado da acceso directo al mar. El interior es un lugar con mucho estilo: la elección de los colores y del mobiliario proporciona un ambiente moderno y distinguido.

Questa magnifica casa è stata costruita nel 1938 come ampliamento di una già esistente. In seguito a dei lavori di ristrutturazione per adattarla al clima della zona, gli attuali proprietari l'hanno trasformata nella loro abituale residenza. All'esterno troviamo una fantastica piscina, un portico con un'accogliente sala da pranzo e delle comode sdraio di design. Grazie a un molo privato si accede direttamente al mare. Gli interni sono stati arredati con gusto ed eleganza.

Architect: Warren Ser (remodelling)
Interior design: Alison Spear, Tom Healy and Fred Hochberg
Photographer: © Reto Guntli / Zapaimages

The pool area is the ideal place to enjoy the Miami climate. The large terrace has access to the upper terrace as well as the porch. There are many leisure and relaxation options available to enjoy a great lifestyle.

Am Swimmingpool kann man das milde Klima Miamis genießen. Von der großen Terrasse gibt es einen Zugang zu einer weitläufigen oberen Terrasse. Hier kann man vielen verschiedenen Aktivitäten nachgehen und das Leben auf ganz besondere Art genießen.

La zone de la piscine est le lieu idéal pour jouir du climat de Miami. La grande terrasse compte un accès à la vaste terrasse supérieure. De multiples possibilités de loisirs et de repos permettent de profiter d'un merveilleux style de vie.

El área de la piscina es el lugar ideal para disfrutar del clima de Miami. La gran terraza cuenta con un acceso a una amplia terraza superior. Las posibilidades de ocio y descanso son múltiples y permiten disfrutar de un maravilloso estilo de vida.

L'area che accoglie la piscina è il luogo ideale dove godersi tranquillamente il clima di Miami. La grande terrazza dispone di un accesso ad un'ampia terrazza superiore. In quest'ambiente le possibilità di svago e di relax sono varie.

The bedrooms have each been decorated in a different and individual style. The main bedroom breathes elegance and eminence thanks to the green color of one of the walls, the robust headboard and the bedside table lamps. In the main bathroom the light and spaciousness confer modernity and style to the space.

Jedes der Schlafzimmer wurde anders dekoriert, so dass jedes originell und sehr individuell gestaltet ist. Im großen Schlafzimmer schufen die Gestalter mit der grünen Wand, dem robusten Kopfteil des Bettes und den Nachttischlampen eine edle und elegante Atmosphäre. Das Hauptbadezimmer, das hell und groß ist, ist ebenfalls ein sehr moderner und stilvoller Raum.

Les chambres sont décorées indépendamment les unes des autres, chacune ayant sa particularité qui la rend originale. Dans la chambre de maître, la couleur verte de l'un des murs, la solide tête de lit et les lampes des tables de nuit créent une ambiance élégante et distinguée. Dans la salle de bains principale, la lumière et l'espace ample confèrent modernité et style à l'espace.

Los dormitorios se han decorado de forma independiente, pues cada uno tiene una particularidad que lo hace original. En el dormitorio principal, el color verde de una de las paredes, el robusto cabezal y las lámparas en las mesillas de noche crean un ambiente elegante y distinguido. En el baño principal la luz y la amplitud otorgan al espacio modernidad y estilo.

Le camere da letto presentano arredamenti diversi, ognuna con degli elementi che la caratterizzano. In quella principale, ad esempio, il verde di una delle pareti, il robusto capezzale e le lampade dei comodini creano un ambiente elegante e raffinato. Nel bagno principale l'ampiezza e la luce conferiscono una certa dose di modernità allo spazio.

On the quay there is a small dining area which makes it an ideal place to enjoy the sounds of the surf. The garden which borders the dwelling is designed by landscape architect Robert Parsley and Geomantic Designs. It successfully recreates a tropical and relaxing atmosphere.

Am Landesteg befindet sich eine kleine Essgelegenheit, wo man direkt am Wasser speisen kann. Der Garten ist ein Werk des Landschaftsarchitekten Robert Parsley und von Geomantic Designs. Er umgibt das Haus und schafft eine tropische und entspannte Atmosphäre.

Le ponton a vu l'installation d'une petite salle à manger qui en fait le lieu idéal pour profiter de la proximité de l'eau. Le jardin, œuvre de l'architecte paysagiste Robert Parsley pour Geomantic Designs, entoure la demeure et crée une atmosphère tropicale et relaxante.

En el muelle se ha instalado un pequeño comedor que lo convierte en el lugar perfecto para disfrutar de la proximidad del agua. El jardín, obra del paisajista Robert Parsley y Geomantic Designs, está situado alrededor de la vivienda y consigue recrear una atmósfera tropical y relajante.

Presso il molo è stato allestito un piccolo angolo pranzo che permette di degustare i vari pasti stando quasi a contatto con l'acqua. Il giardino, opera del paesaggista Robert Parsley e Geomantic Designs, circonda tutta l'abitazione e riesce a ricreare un'atmosfera tropicale e rilassante.

Residence in Miami

Miami, USA

Miami is an ideal place to enjoy the good climate and the proximity of the ocean. This dwelling of traditional and elegant architectonic lines is a perfect example, with a neat garden at the front and a pool and quay at the rear. The round shaped staircase separates the private rooms on the upper floor from the living room and day areas downstairs. Outside, a delightful pool synchronizes with the ocean as only a thin stretch of land separates them.

Miami eignet sich wunderbar dazu, das angenehme Klima am Meer zu genießen. Dieses Haus zeigt sich in einer eleganten und traditionellen Bauweise, es verfügt über einen Vorgarten, einen Swimmingpool und einen Steg hinter dem Haus. Die elegante Treppe mit abgerundeten Linien führt in die privateren Räume im Obergeschoss, während die Wohnzimmer und die tagsüber genutzten Räume im unteren Geschoss liegen. Draußen vor dem Haus geht ein wundervoller Swimmingpool beinahe in das Meer über, von dem er nur durch eine schmale Landzunge getrennt ist.

Miami est un endroit idéal où jouir d'un climat agréable et de l'océan tout proche. Celle-çi en particulier affiche une architecture élégante et traditionnelle et inclut un jardin soigné à l'entrée, ainsi qu'une zone de piscine et un ponton à l'arrière. L'escalier stylisé aux lignes arrondies mène aux pièces privées du niveau supérieur, et aux salons ainsi qu'aux zones diurnes du niveau inférieur. À l'extérieur de la maison, une magnifique piscine se confond avec l'océan, dont elle est séparée par une étroite bande de sol.

Miami es el lugar idóneo para disfrutar de un clima agradable y de la cercanía del océano. Esta residencia muestra una arquitectura elegante y tradicional, e incluye un cuidado jardín en la entrada, una zona con piscina y un muelle en la parte posterior. La elegante escalera de líneas redondeadas conduce a las estancias privadas en el piso superior, y a los salones y las zonas de día en el nivel inferior. En el exterior de la vivienda, una magnífica piscina se confunde con el océano, del que se halla separada por una estrecha lengua de tierra.

Miami è la città idonea per godere di un clima particolarmente favorevole e della prossimità dell'oceano. Questa villa, che presenta un'architettura elegante e al contempo tradizionale, comprende all'ingresso un giardino ben curato, una zona con piscina e un piccolo molo nella parte posteriore. L'elegante scala dalle linee arrotondate porta alla sala e alle zone giorno nel livello inferiore e alle stanze private della zona notte al piano superiore. All'esterno, l'abitazione dispone di una magnifica piscina che si confonde quasi con l'oceano, dal quale la separa solo una stretta striscia di terra.

Architect: Wallace Tutt / Tutt Renovation & Development
Photographer: © Pep Escoda

The living room is a distinguished and elegant room. *The careful and sophisticated distribution of the space and furniture makes for a stylish ambience. The choice of sofas and armchairs along with the mirrors, the stucco and the chimney, create a fascinating room.*

Das Wohnzimmer ist elegant und geschmackvoll gestaltet. *Die gelungene Raumaufteilung und die edlen Möbel erzeugen ein stilvolles und luxuriöses Ambiente, und die Spiegel, der Stuck, der Kamin und die eleganten Sofas und Sessel schaffen einen interessanten Raum.*

Le salon est une pièce élégante et distinguée. *D'un côté, la distribution recherchée de l'espace et du mobilier confère élégance et style à l'ensemble ; de l'autre, les miroirs, les séduisantes moulures du plafond, la cheminée et le choix judicieux de sofas et fauteuils contribuent à créer une pièce fascinante.*

El salón es una estancia elegante y distinguida. *Por un lado, la cuidada distribución del espacio y del mobiliario otorga elegancia y estilo al ambiente; por otro, los espejos, el estuco, la chimenea y la acertada elección de sofás y butacas contribuyen a crear una estancia fascinante.*

Il salone è arredato con eleganza e buon gusto. *Da una parte, l'accurata distribuzione dello spazio e della mobilia trasmette eleganza e stile all'ambiente; dall'altra, gli specchi, lo stucco, il camino e l'azzeccata selezione di poltrone e divani aiutano a creare una stanza dall'estetica raffinata.*

The pool and private quay are located in a space with real holiday spirit. The sea and sun allows the owners full enjoyment of the fresh air and the many activities available, from relaxing on the sun beds to a quick spin on the motor boat.

Der Swimmingpool und der private Anlegesteg gehören zu den Gartenanlagen des Hauses. Das Meer und die Sonne bilden den perfekten Rahmen für den Aufenthalt im Freien, den man einfach nur entspannt im Liegestuhl genießen oder zu einer kleinen Bootsfahrt nutzen kann.

La piscine et le ponton privé forment partie de la zone récréative de la résidence. La mer et le soleil créent un cadre parfait pour prendre du bon temps à l'air libre, avec de multiples possibilités de divertissement et de repos, du bain de soleil sur les transats à l'escapade en bateau.

La piscina y el muelle privado forman parte de la zona recreativa de la residencia. El mar y el sol proporcionan el marco perfecto para disfrutar al aire libre, con múltiples posibilidades para divertirse y descansar, desde tomar el sol en las tumbonas hasta disfrutar de un paseo en lancha.

La zona ricreativa della residenza comprende la piscina e il molo privato. Quest'ultimo si trasforma in punto di partenza di piacevoli gite a bordo di lance o altre imbarcazioni da diporto o in una comoda zona relax dove sdraiarsi all'aria aperta a prendere il sole.

Stinson Beach

Northern California, USA

Although this house is a second residence on the coast, the interior has a more urban and cosmopolitan ambience. The owners spend more time in the beach house than in their main home in San Francisco and therefore prefer this kind of design. The rooms are decorated with an elegant mix of the owners' favorite styles—contemporary, classic and Asiatic. The collection of contemporary art also confers a special importance as well as the other materials in the house. The result is a high quality, splendid and original dwelling beside the sea.

Dieses Haus, eigentlich ein Ferienhaus am Meer, wirkt im Inneren eher urban und kosmopolitisch. Das wünschten die Eigentümer sich so, denn sie verbringen mehr Zeit in ihrem Haus am Strand als an ihrem Hauptwohnsitz in San Francisco. In den Räumen findet man eine elegante Mischung der Stile, die die Eigentümer bevorzugen, nämlich modern, klassisch und asiatisch. Auch die Sammlung zeitgenössischer Kunst ist ausschlaggebend für die Atmosphäre der Räume, ebenso wie die verwendeten Materialien. So entstand ein wundervolles Haus am Meer, das sehr schön, originell und elegant gestaltet ist.

Cette maison est en fait une résidence secondaire située sur la côte, mais ses intérieurs rappellent une ambiance urbaine et cosmopolite. C'était le souhait des propriétaires, qui passent plus de temps dans leur maison de plage que dans leur résidence principale de San Francisco. Les pièces ont été décorées avec un mélange élégant des styles préférés des propriétaires : contemporain, classique et asiatique. La collection d'art contemporain joue également un rôle spécial, comme les matériaux de la maison. Il en résulte une splendide demeure au bord de la mer, séduisante, originale et de grande qualité.

Esta casa es en realidad una segunda residencia situada en la costa, pero su interior recuerda un ambiente urbano y cosmopolita. Éste era el deseo de los propietarios, quienes pasan más tiempo en la casa de la playa que en su principal vivienda de la ciudad de San Francisco. Las estancias se decoraron con una elegante mezcla de los estilos preferidos de los propietarios: contemporáneo, clásico y asiático. La colección de arte contemporáneo también adquiere un especial protagonismo, al igual que otros materiales de la casa. El resultado es una espléndida vivienda junto al mar muy atractiva, original y de gran calidad.

L'arredamento interno di questa casa situata nella costa ricorda un ambiente urbano e cosmopolita. Questo è stato infatti il desiderio dei suoi proprietari che trascorrono più tempo in questa residenza di villeggiatura che nella loro abitazione della città di San Francisco. Le varie stanze sono state arredate con un'elegante mescolanza di stili: contemporaneo, classico ed asiatico. Tra i vari elementi di arredo della casa, spicca una collezione di opere d'arte contemporanea. Nel complesso si tratta di una splendida villa accanto al mare, dotata di stile ed originalità.

Interior design: Sally Sirkin Interior Design
Photographer: © Tim Street-Porter

The exterior part of the house is also a contemporary and elegant space. The construction lines are extremely clean and create a truly ethereal atmosphere. Sizeable windows in the first floor rooms allow for spectacular views of the ocean.

Auch die Außenbereiche sind in einem modernen und eleganten Stil gehalten. Die architektonischen Linien sind sehr klar und lassen eine sehr edle Atmosphäre entstehen. Die Räume im ersten Stock haben große Fenster, von denen aus man einen wundervollen Blick auf den Ozean genießt.

L'extérieur de la maison est aussi un espace contemporain et élégant. Les lignes de la construction sont extrêmement épurées, et créent une atmosphère d'une grande délicatesse. Les pièces du premier niveau proposent également de grandes baies vitrées, depuis lesquelles on peut jouir de vues spectaculaires sur l'océan.

El exterior de la casa también es un espacio contemporáneo y elegante. Las líneas constructivas son extremadamente limpias y crean una atmósfera de gran delicadeza. En las estancias del primer piso también se encuentran grandes ventanales desde los que disfrutar de espectaculares vistas al océano.

Anche l'esterno della casa è uno spazio elegante dalle linee contemporanee. La sobrietà delle costruzioni dà vita a un'atmosfera alquanto delicata. Al primo piano le stanze dispongono di ampie vetrate con magnifiche viste panoramiche sull'oceano.

The contemporary art paintings and sculptures are exceptional in this residence and proclaim the owners' good taste and knowledge. The result is a distinguished, warm luxurious house.

Die zeitgenössischen Bilder und Skulpturen sind die auffallendsten Elemente in den Räumen, sie zeigen den guten Geschmack und die umfassenden Kunstkenntnisse der Eigentümer. Das Haus wirkt edel und freundlich und gleichzeitig strahlt es eine zurückhaltende Pracht aus.

Tableaux et sculptures d'art contemporain se distinguent d'une pièce à l'autre de la résidence et soulignent le goût et la culture des propriétaires : en naît une maison distinguée, chaleureuse, à la somptuosité mesurée.

Los cuadros y esculturas de arte contemporáneo destacan entre las estancias de la residencia y ponen de manifiesto el gusto y conocimiento de los propietarios. El resultado es una casa distinguida, cálida y con una comedida suntuosidad.

I quadri e le sculture di arte contemporanea abbelliscono le varie stanze ed evidenziano il gusto e le conoscenze artistiche dei proprietari. Il risultato è una casa raffinata, accogliente, dalla sontuosità misurata.

Beach Front Home

Punta del Este, Uruguay

Punta del Este is a privileged corner of the Atlantic coast boasting miles and miles of rocky outcrops and long sandy beaches. This peninsula is a popular tourist destination although its elite nature helps to keep the crowds at bay. This residence is a good example of how architecture is able to adapt itself to magnificent surroundings. The proximity of the beaches and the ocean encourages the construction of wide open spaces. The architecture combines elegant lines, free from excesses and ostentation, with an uncomplicated rustic decoration bringing simplicity and distinction to the interiors.

Punta del Este ist ein besonders schöner Ort an der Atlantikküste. Auf dem kilometerlangen Küstenabschnitt wechseln sich Felsküsten mit großen Stränden ab. Diese Halbinsel ist ein beliebtes Touristenziel, das jedoch so elitär ist, dass man viel Ruhe an den Stränden findet. Dieses Haus ist ein gutes Beispiel dafür, wie man die Architektur an eine wundervolle Umgebung anpassen kann. Da die Strände und der Ozean so nah liegen, schuf man große, offene Räume. Die architektonischen Linien sind sehr elegant, ohne Übertreibung oder Zurschaustellung, und die Dekoration ist einfach, leicht rustikal, so dass die Räume schlicht und gleichzeitig sehr edel wirken.

La Punta del Este est un lieu privilégié de la côte atlantique : les kilomètres de côte se succèdent, alternant zones rocheuses et vastes plages. Cette péninsule est une destination touristique de choix, mais son caractère élitiste permet de jouir des plages avec tranquillité. Cette résidence est un bon exemple de la façon dont l'architecture peut s'adapter à un cadre magnifique. La proximité des plages et de l'océan incite à la construction de grands espaces ouverts. L'architecture propose des lignes élégantes, sans excès ni ostentation, et la décoration est simple avec une touche rustique offrant naturel et distinction aux intérieurs.

Punta del Este es un lugar privilegiado de la costa atlántica; kilómetros y kilómetros de costa se suceden alternando zonas rocosas con extensas playas. Esta península es un destino turístico muy concurrido, aunque su carácter elitista permite disfrutar de las playas con tranquilidad. Esta residencia es un claro ejemplo de cómo la arquitectura puede adaptarse a un magnífico entorno; la cercanía de las playas y del océano propicia la construcción de grandes espacios abiertos. La arquitectura es de líneas elegantes, sin excesos ni ostentación, y la decoración es sencilla, con un toque rústico que confiere a los interiores sencillez y distinción a la vez.

Punta del Este è un luogo privilegiato della costa atlantica; chilometri di costa si susseguono alternando zone rocciose a vasti litorali sabbiosi. Questa penisola è una meta turistica molto frequentata, sebbene il suo carattere elitario consente di godere delle spiagge con relativa tranquillità. Questa residenza è un chiaro esempio di come l'architettura possa adattarsi ad un magnifico ambiente circostante; la vicinanza delle spiagge e dell'oceano propizia la costruzione di grandi spazi aperti. Le linee architettoniche sono eleganti, prive di eccessi ed ostentazione mentre l'arredamento è molto essenziale, con dei tocchi rustici che danno agli interni semplicità e al contempo una certa distinzione.

Architect: Martín Gómez
Photographer: © Ricardo Labougle

The swimming pool and porch are sited on a level above the beach. The wooden fences surrounding the house and the deck next to the swimming pool bring warmth to the environment. The first floor windows offer spectacular views over the Atlantic Ocean.

Der Swimmingpool und die Veranda liegen etwas über der Höhe des Strandes. Durch das Holz des Zaunes, der das Grundstück umgibt, und des Bodens am Pool entsteht eine natürliche und einladende Atmosphäre. Von den Fenstern der ersten Etage aus überblickt man den fast unendlichen Atlantischen Ozean.

La piscine et la véranda sont légèrement surélevés par rapport à la plage. Le bois de la clôture entourant le lieu et le lambris autour la piscine créent une ambiance naturelle et accueillante. Les fenêtres au premier offrent des vues quasi infinies sur l'Atlantique.

La piscina y el porche se encuentran ligeramente elevados sobre el nivel de la playa. La madera de la valla que rodea la finca y de la tarima que hay junto a la piscina crea un ambiente natural y acogedor, y las ventanas del primer piso ofrecen unas vistas al océano Atlántico casi infinitas.

La piscina e il portico si trovano in una posizione leggermente elevata rispetto al livello della spiaggia. Il legno dello steccato che circonda la tenuta e della pedana sita accanto alla piscina crea un ambiente naturale ed accogliente; le finestre del primo piano offrono delle vedute quasi infinite dell'oceano Atlantico.

The combination of warm and cold elements make the interior of the house an elegant space; the stone and wood of the walls contrast well with the concrete floor and create a space with a unique atmosphere. The wooden beams are another important characteristic feature of the house.

Die Räume sind sehr elegant, hier wurden warme und kühle Elemente miteinander kombiniert. Die Natursteine und das Holz an den Wänden kontrastieren mit dem Betonboden, so dass ein Raum mit einer sehr eigenen Atmosphäre entstanden ist. Das Dach mit Holzbalken ist ein anderes Element, das dieses Haus einzigartig macht.

L'intérieur de la demeure est un espace élégant, fruit de la combinaison d'éléments chauds et froids : la pierre et le bois des murs contrastent avec le sol en béton pour créer un espace doté d'une atmosphère propre. La couverte de poutres de bois est un autre élément assurant la singularité de la maison.

El interior de la vivienda es un espacio elegante, fruto de una combinación de elementos cálidos y fríos; la piedra y la madera en las paredes contrastan con el suelo de hormigón y crea un espacio con atmósfera propia. La cubierta de vigas de madera es otro de los elementos que aportan singularidad a la casa.

L'interno dell'abitazione è uno spazio elegante, frutto di una combinazione di elementi caldi e freddi; la pietra e il legno delle pareti contrastano con il pavimento in cemento, creando uno spazio dalla peculiare atmosfera. Il soffitto con le travi in legno è un altro degli elementi che apportano singolarità alla casa.

Calm Sea

Punta del Este, Uruguay

The location of this magnificent dwelling, which is completely isolated on the beach results in a charming refuge, far from the worries and stress of daily life. Calm and tranquility pervade all corners of this residence. The house is designed with a very fluid spatial distribution given that each room has an exit outdoors. An interior space, where the terrace and pool are located, is in the centre of the dwelling. Lapacha wood, which is as resistant as teak, has been used for the exterior areas. The interior is decorated with elegant furniture from Syria, Armenia and India which results in a relaxed and comfortable atmosphere.

Dieses bezaubernde Haus liegt völlig einsam am Strand, ein wundervoller Zufluchtsort, an dem man die täglichen Sorgen und den Stress vergessen kann. Ruhe und Frieden durchdringen jeden Winkel des Hauses. Die Raumaufteilung ist sehr fließend und man gelangt von überall ins Freie. Ein innerer Raum mit Swimmingpool und Terrasse ist das Zentrum des Hauses. In den Außenbereichen verwendete man Lapacho-Holz, das genauso widerstandsfähig wie Teakholz ist. Die Räume sind mit eleganten Möbeln aus Syrien, Armenien und Indien dekoriert, die eine entspannte und komfortable Atmosphäre entstehen lassen.

L'emplacement de cette magnifique demeure, complètement isolée sur la plage, en fait un refuge enchanteur, loin des soucis et du stress quotidiens. Le calme et la tranquillité investissent chaque recoin de la résidence. La maison est pensée selon une distribution spatiale très fluide : l'extérieur est accessible depuis chaque pièce. Un espace intérieur, accueillant la piscine et une terrasse, est au cœur de la demeure. Du bois de lapacho, aussi résistant que le teck, a été employé pour les zones extérieures. L'intérieur est décoré de meubles élégants, provenant de Syrie, d'Arménie ou d'Inde, qui créent une atmosphère détendue et confortable.

La localización de esta magnífica vivienda, completamente aislada en la playa, la convierte en un encantador refugio, lejos de las preocupaciones diarias y del estrés. La calma y la tranquilidad invaden todos los rincones de la residencia. La casa está diseñada con una distribución espacial muy fluida, pues desde cualquier estancia se puede acceder al exterior. Un espacio interior, donde se ubica la piscina y una terraza, es el centro de la vivienda. Para las zonas exteriores, se ha utilizado la madera de lapacho, tan resistente como la de teca. El interior está decorado con elegantes muebles, procedentes de Siria, Armenia o la India, que crean una atmósfera relajada y confortable.

Questa magnifica dimora è situata in una zona un po' appartata del litorale. La quiete del posto la trasforma in un piacevole rifugio, lontano dalle preoccupazioni e dallo stress quotidiano. La casa presenta una distribuzione spaziale molto fluida; da qualsiasi stanza è infatti possibile accedere all'esterno. Uno spazio interno, che accoglie la piscina e una terrazza, è il vero centro dell'abitazione. Per le zone esterne è stato utilizzato il lapaco, resistente e duraturo come il tek. Gli interni sono stati arredati con mobili eleganti di provenienza orientale - Siria, Armenia, India – che creano un'atmosfera serena e confortevole.

Architect: Mario Connío
Photographer: © Ricardo Labougle

The bedroom and bathrooms combine natural materials to create a sense of warmth. The ceramics of the bathroom, the stone wall and the original ceiling fan add a personal touch to the decoration.

In den Schlafzimmern und Bädern wurden natürliche Materialien miteinander kombiniert, um eine warme Atmosphäre zu schaffen. Die Kacheln im Bad, die Wand aus Naturstein und der originelle Deckenventilator lassen die Einrichtung sehr persönlich wirken.

La chambre et les salles de bain combinent matériaux nobles afin de créer une ambiance chaleureuse. La céramique, la paroi de pierre et le ventilateur original qui se trouve au plafond dotent la décoration de beaucoup de personalité.

El dormitorio y los baños combinan los materiales naturales para crear ambientes cálidos. La cerámica del baño, la pared de piedra y el original ventilador en el techo aportan personalidad a la decoración.

Anche nelle stanze da letto e nei bagni si combinano i materiali naturali per creare ambienti accoglienti. La ceramica del bagno, la parete in pietra e l'originale ventilatore del soffitto danno personalità all'arredamento.

The exterior walls have been covered with traditional stucco which does not require special maintenance. The terracotta color combines perfectly with the colors of the sand and helps blend the house into the landscape.

Die Außenwände sind mit dem traditionellen Stuck der Region bedeckt, der keine besondere Pflege benötigt. Das Terrakotta passt perfekt zu den Sandtönen und integriert das Haus in die Landschaft.

Les murs extérieurs ont été couverts de stuc traditionnel, ne requérant aucun entretien spécial. La couleur ocre se marie à la perfection avec les tonalités du sable et permet d'intégrer la maison dans le paysage.

Las paredes exteriores se han cubierto con un estuco tradicional que no requiere especial mantenimiento. El color terracota escogido combina a la perfección con los tonos de la arena y permite la integración de la casa en el paisaje.

Le pareti esterne sono state ricoperte da stucco tradizionale, un materiale che non richiede una particolare manutenzione. Il colore terracotta combina alla perfezione con le tonalità della sabbia e agevola l'integrazione della casa nel paesaggio.

The pool and the porch *form a central space with the bedrooms and living rooms arranged around it. This arrangement makes for a special relationship between the rooms in that they all have exits outside. The terrace, the hammocks next to the water and the blinds which define the spaces create a fluid interior area in contrast with the robust exterior architectural lines.*

Der Swimmingpool und die Veranda *bilden einen zentralen Raum, um den herum die Schlaf- und Wohnzimmer liegen. Durch diese Aufteilung entstand eine ganz besondere Beziehung zwischen den Räumen, die sich alle nach außen öffnen. Die Terrasse, die Liegestühle am Wasser und die Jalousien, die die Bereiche begrenzen, schaffen einen fließenden inneren Raum, der zu den robusten architektonischen Linien des Gebäudeäußeren im Gegensatz steht.*

La piscine et la véranda *forment un espace central entouré des chambres et des salles de séjour. Cette distribution établit une relation spéciale entre les pièces, toutes ouvertes sur l'extérieur. La terrasse, les hamacs au bord de l'eau et les persiennes délimitant les espaces créent une zone intérieure fluide, qui contraste avec les solides lignes architecturales extérieures.*

La piscina y el porche *forman un espacio central que dispone a su alrededor los dormitorios y las salas de estar. Esta distribución permite establecer una relación especial entre las estancias, todas ellas abiertas al exterior. La terraza, las hamacas junto al agua y las persianas que delimitan los espacios crean un lugar interior fluido que contrasta con las robustas líneas arquitectónicas exteriores.*

La piscina e il portico *formano uno spazio centrale attorno a cui si dispongono le camere da letto e le zone soggiorno. Questo tipo di distribuzione stabilisce una relazione speciale fra le stanze, tutte esposte all'esterno. La terrazza, i lettini accanto all'acqua e le persiane che delimitano gli spazi creano un luogo interno fluido che contrasta con le robuste linee architettoniche esterne.*

The interior of the residence is decorated with a mix of very personal styles. Some simple rooms exist side by side with others more exuberant and lavish. In the main room, for example, the comfortable and elegant sofas and magnificent maps and sculptures lend a rather majestic air to the space.

Die Räume des Hauses sind in einer sehr persönlichen Mischung verschiedener Stile dekoriert. Einfachere Räume wechseln sich mit prunkvollen und pompösen Dekorationen ab. Im großen Wohnzimmer fallen zum Beispiel die eleganten und komfortablen Sofas und die wundervollen Karten und Skulpturen auf, die eine herrschaftliche Atmosphäre entstehen lassen.

L'intérieur de la résidence est décoré d'un mélange de styles très personnels. Des pièces plus simples coexistent avec d'autres plus exubérantes et fastueuses. Dans la salle principale, par exemple, se distinguent d'élégants et confortables sofas et de magnifiques plans et sculptures, qui confèrent à l'espace une atmosphère majestueuse.

El interior de la residencia está decorado con una mezcla de estilos muy personal. Unas estancias más sencillas conviven con otras más exuberantes y fastuosas. En la sala principal, por ejemplo, destacan los elegantes y confortables sofás y los magníficos mapas y esculturas, que otorgan al espacio una atmósfera majestuosa.

L'interno della residenza è arredato con una mescolanza di stili molto personale. Alcune stanze più semplici convivono con altre, più esuberanti e fastose. Nella sala principale, ad esempio, spiccano eleganti e comodi divani, cartine e sculture di pregevole fattura, che danno allo spazio un tocco di voluta maestosità.

Materials common to local architecture have been used throughout the residence. For example, the roofing of the towers have been built with "quincho", a type of reed which helps maintain a cool temperature in summer and warm in winter, as well as creating a very cozy atmosphere.

Im ganzen Haus wurden Materialien benutzt, die typisch für die regionale Architektur sind. So sind zum Beispiel die Decken der Türme aus Quincho, einer Schilfrohrart, die die Räume im Sommer gegen Hitze und im Winter gegen Kälte schützt und gleichzeitig eine sehr warme Atmosphäre schafft.

Dans toute la résidence, les matériaux propres à l'architecture locale ont été employés. Ainsi, les toits des tours ont été construits en quincho, une canne qui permet de maintenir une température fraîche en été et chaude en hiver, tout en faisant conférant une atmosphère très accueillante.

En toda la residencia se han utilizado materiales propios de la arquitectura local. Por ejemplo, los techos de las torres están construidos con quincho, una caña que ayuda a mantener la temperatura fresca en verano y cálida en invierno, al tiempo que crea una atmósfera muy acogedora.

In tutta la casa sono stati adoperati materiali tipici dell'architettura locale. Ad esempio, i tetti delle torri sono stati rivestiti da "quincho", una fitta stuoia di canne che aiuta a mantenere una temperatura fresca in estate e calda in inverno e che crea, allo stesso tempo, un ambiente accogliente.

| *Editor and texts:* | Cristina Paredes Benítez |

| *Art Director:* | Mireia Casanovas Soley |

| *Layout:* | Elisabet Rodríguez, Luis F. Sierra, Zahira Rodríguez Mediavilla |

Translations:	Enrique Góngora Padilla (English)
	Marion Westerhoff (French)
	Martin Fischer (German)
	Donatella Talpo (Italian)

Produced by Loft Publications
www.loftpublications.com

Published by teNeues Publishing Group

teNeues Publishing Company
16 West 22nd Street, New York, NY 10010, USA
Tel.: 001-212-627-9090, Fax: 001-212-627-9511

teNeues Verlag GmbH + Co. KG
International Sales Division
Speditionsstr. 17, 40221 Düsseldorf, Germany
Tel.: 0049-(0)211-994597-0, Fax: 0049-(0)211-994597-40

teNeues Publishing UK Ltd.
P.O. Box 402, West Byfleet, KT14 7ZF, Great Britain
Tel.: 0044-1932-403509, Fax: 0044-1932-403514

teNeues France S.A.R.L.
4, rue de Valence, 75005 Paris, France
Tel.: 0033-1-55 76 62 05, Fax: 0033-1-55 76 64 19

teNeues Ibérica S.L.
c/ Velázquez, 57 6.º izda.
28001 Madrid, Spain
Tel.: 0034-(0)657 132133

teNeues Representative Office Italy
Via San Vittore 36/1
20123 Milano, Italy
Tel.: 0039-(0)347-76 40 551

www.teneues.com

| ISBN-10: | 3-8327-9109-4 |
| ISBN-13: | 978-3-8327-9109-4 |

© 2006 teNeues Verlag GmbH + Co. KG, Kempen

Printed in Spain

Bibliographic information published by
Die Deutsche Bibliothek. Die Deutsche Bibliothek lists
this publication in the Deutsche Nationalbibliografie;
detailed bibliographic data is available in the Internet